Living with a
Sporting Spaniel

© D. Shields

Edited by Julia Barnes

BARRON'S

THE QUESTION OF GENDER
The "he" pronoun is used throughout this book in favor of the rather impersonal "it," but no gender bias is intended.

ACKNOWLEDGMENTS

The publisher would like to thank the following for use of their beautiful photographs: Donna and David Shields (D & D Imaging); Annalies Roeterdink; Eileen Speich; Jill Holgate (Field Spaniel Society); Deborah Hughes (Ildanoch Irish Water Spaniels); Ann McGloon (Shooting Star Sussex Spaniels); Arlene Tester (AVILT Welsh Springer Spaniels); Shannon T. Rodgers; Lara and Richard Suesens (Wave Crest American Water Spaniels, http://wavecrestaws.tripod.com); Jeane Haverick (Clussexx Clumber Spaniels); Jackie Crawford, Abbyford Clumber Spaniels (www.abbyford.co.uk); Jim Zimmerlin (www.zimfamilycockers.com); Larry and Mary Joan Kunkle; Shannon McCracken; Linda Ford (California American Water Spaniels); William and Cindy Brizes; Danae Steel; Kerry Stevenson; Bea Chugkowski; Janet Martin (Ariel English Springers); Michelle Givens (Wilden English Springers); Arlene Cohen; Betty Watne; Karen Cottingham (Prime Time Sussex Spaniels); Sally Abrahms.
Thanks are also due to Neal Winters (Fox River Field Spaniel Club) and Mary Parszewski (English Springer Spaniel Field Trial Association) for their help.

First edition for the United States and Canada published
2006 by Barron's Educational Series, Inc.

Designed by Sarah Williams

First published in Great Britain in 2006 by Westline Publishing Ltd

© 2006 Westline Publishing Ltd
(A division of Interpet Publishing)

All inquiries should be addressed to:
Barron's Educational Series, Inc.
250 Wireless Boulevard, Hauppauge, NY 11788
http://www.barronseduc.com

ISBN-13: 978-0-7641-5859-9
ISBN-10: 0-7641-5859-7

Library of Congress Control Number 2004113931

PRINTED IN CHINA

0 9 8 7 6 5 4 3 2 1

CONTENTS

CHAPTER ONE

INTRODUCING SPORTING SPANIELS

Merry, tail-wagging, docile, and sweet natured, Spaniels come in many different shapes and sizes, but there are a number of characteristics that unite them. Perhaps the most important of all is that Spaniels were bred to work closely with their owners, and this desire for human companionship is one of the most endearing traits that is shared by all breeds of Spaniel.

SPORTING HISTORY

Spaniels have been around for a long time—at least 700–800 years. The name "Spaniel' comes from "Hispanola," which is old Spanish for "Spain," or from "espaignol," which is old French for "Spanish Dog." It is therefore thought that Spaniels originally came from Spain, and when the Romans traveled through Europe, expanding the Roman Empire, many dog breeds became more widespread.

The earliest literary references date back to Chaucer in *The Wife of Bath's Tale*, and a Spaniel also crops up in Shakespeare's *King Lear*.

However, the first attempt to classify Spaniels comes around 1570 when Dr. John Caius compiled his book *Of Englishe Dogges*. He split Spaniels into the bigger types who were used for retrieving, mostly in water, and smaller types who worked on the land. However, it is clear that, from the earliest times, Spaniels excelled at locating, flushing out, and retrieving all types of small game.

The Spaniel worked in a distinctive manner, quartering the field (working in a zigzag pattern), and then sniffing out game within gun range and flushing it out. The Spaniel had to sit while the guns were fired and was then sent off to retrieve the game, regardless of whether it had fallen on land or in water.

In an article published in the 1880s, Spaniels were described in the following way:

The Spaniel was chosen above all other dogs, more than 250 years ago, for his generous and grateful nature, as an example to mankind, and to the present time these good qualifications have not degenerated, for he stands out boldly, the most useful, grateful and companionable to mankind, Nature was generous in giving such a creature to man, for him to form and cultivate into such a beautiful and useful animal.

He is small yet large, in symmetry perfection; head beautifully moulded and beaming with intelligence; neck muscular for retrieving and body well balanced on short, straight, strong legs. He can be easily and highly trained and beside his own work of finding and flushing all kinds of game in the thickest covers, or in open fields, he is equal to the Retriever on land or water, and can fill the gap of a Setter or a Pointer with credit.

ADVENT OF DOG SHOWS

On the large country estates in England and Scotland, dogs were bred specifically as shooting companions, and the emphasis was on producing a type of dog that would particularly suit local conditions. Records were kept of the bloodlines used, and this led to the creation of a number of breeds, including the Clumber Spaniel and the Sussex Spaniel.

It was with the start of dog shows, though, and the formation of the Kennel Club in 1873 that efforts were made to categorize types of dogs into specific breeds. One of the early clubs was the Sporting Spaniel Club, which was founded in the 1880s. Its first meeting was at the Bull Hotel in Woodbridge, Suffolk, U.K., and the aim was to arrange competitive matches in the field for hunting Spaniels. It is highly likely that Ernest Wells, who later emigrated to the United States and set up the famous Mahwire Kennel of English Springer Spaniels, was among those present.

AMERICAN INFLUENCE

The first Spaniels reached the United States in the early 1800s, and they soon became valued as versatile hunting dogs. They were often to be found in small settlements close to game areas. Spaniels generally worked in swamplands or in thick bramble cover, hunting and retrieving wildfowl and partridge.

The American Spaniel Club was founded in 1881. Over a period of time, sporting Spaniels were recognized as individual breeds.

SPORTING SPANIELS TODAY

There are now nine breeds of Spaniel recognized by the American Kennel Club. They are classified in the Sporting Group and include the American Water Spaniel, the American Cocker

The English Cocker Spaniel: A sporting dog that is alive with energy.

The Sussex Spaniel: The breed's short legs, massive build, long body, and habit of giving its tongue when on a scent made it ideal for flushing game in thick undergrowth, within range of the gun.

Spaniel (known in the United States as the Cocker Spaniel), the Clumber Spaniel, the English Cocker Spaniel, the English Springer Spaniel, the Field Spaniel, the Irish Water Spaniel, the Sussex Spaniel, and the Welsh Springer Spaniel. In the U.K., the Kennel Club recognizes eight Spaniels in the Gundog Group—the American Water Spaniel is not registered as a breed in the U.K.

Developed from the original hunting Spaniels, each breed has been fine-tuned in order to have the conformation, coat type, and character to carry out a specific task. All the Spaniel breeds are still used as working dogs to a greater or lesser extent, but they have also come into their own as companion dogs. The Spaniel's intelligence, pleasing disposition, and his love of people have made him a great favorite among pet owners.

Each breed has its fans, but some have been more universally adopted than others. The annual registration at the American Kennel Club shows the American Cocker Spaniel as the clear leader—he is the 15th most popular of the 150 breeds in the United States, and the English Springer is also highly rated, coming in as the 27th most popular breed.

In the U.K., the English Cocker Spaniel is a big favorite, followed closely by the English Springer. Interestingly, the American Cocker Spaniel has more registrations than any of the other Spaniel breeds that originate in Britain.

AKC REGISTRATIONS

Ranking	Breed	Registrations
15th	Cocker Spaniel (American)	20,655
27th	English Springer Spaniel	9,128
75th	Cocker Spaniel (English)	1,248
113th	Welsh Springer Spaniel	291
120th	American Water Spaniel	196
121st	Clumber Spaniel	188
132nd	Field Spaniel	133
135th	Irish Water Spaniel	116
137th	Sussex Spaniel	108

U.K. KC REGISTRATIONS

Ranking	Breed	Registrations
3rd	English Cocker Spaniel	14,832
4th	English Springer Spaniel	13,877
65th	American Cocker Spaniel	549
77th	Welsh Springer Spaniel	362
113th	Clumber Spaniel	134
123rd	Irish Water Spaniel	121
143rd	Field Spaniel	75
147th	Sussex Spaniel	68

© D. Shields

The English Springer Spaniel: A proud, upstanding dog who suggests power, endurance, and agility.

The Welsh Springer: An attractive dog, of handy size, built for hard work.

THE DOCKING ISSUE

By tradition, working Spaniels always had their tails docked (shortened), with the exception of the American Water Spaniel and the Irish Water Spaniel. This was done for a very practical reason—Spaniels mostly worked in brambles and in thick undergrowth, and a long, feathered tail would be constantly snarled up and might even risk injury. With the advent of dog shows, breed standards were drawn up, and the docked tail was seen as an integral part of each breed's appearance, complementing its overall shape and balance.

Now docking is outlawed in many European countries, and it is becoming commonplace to see Spaniels with full tails. To date, sporting Spaniels are still exhibited in the ring with docked tails in the U.K. and in the U.S.

THE VERSATILE SPANIEL

The Spaniel has proved himself as a top-quality hunting dog and also as a companion par excellence. The multitalented Spaniel also excels at a number of canine sports and disciplines, proving what a true all-around dog he is.

Canine Good Citizen

This is something that every Spaniel owner can try for. Programs have been designed by the Kennel Club and the American Kennel Club.

Awards are given to dogs who gain a basic level of obedience and good manners. Owners must also be well versed in responsible dog ownership.

Competitive Obedience

Spaniels are intelligent dogs who thrive on a challenge, and a number of breeds, particularly the English Springer and the Irish Water Spaniel, have made their mark on obedience.

This is a precision sport, and accuracy is vital. Dogs are tested on heelwork, stays, distance control, recalls, retrieves, sendaways, and scent discrimination. As dogs graduate through the levels, the tasks become increasingly difficult. In the U.S., an agility section is also added.

Field Trials

You may be content to work with your Spaniel in the field noncompetitively, but for those who aspire to a standard of excellence, field trials are the natural choice. As far as Spaniels are concerned, the English Springer tends to be the most successful, but American Cockers and English Cockers are also eligible to compete in their own events.

The aim of a trial is to set up a hunting situation with planted game birds, and dogs are scored as they find, flush, and retrieve. The judges are looking for style, presentation, and control, and the dog must also show speed and intensity of purpose. The goal is for the dog to win enough points to become a field champion.

Hunting Tests

These tests are designed by the American Kennel Club to show that a dog has reached a certain level of performance rather than competing against other dogs to gain maximum points. The areas that are tested include:
• Steady on line
• Quartering
• Finding and flushing birds
• Marking downed birds
• Retrieving on land
• Retrieving from water
• Steadiness to gunfire.

As you graduate through the tests—junior hunter, senior hunter, master hunter—more precision and control are required.

Working Certificate

This scheme presents a great opportunity to keep your Spaniel's working ability intact without the rigorous training that is needed in order to compete in the other field events. Run by individual breed clubs, the working certificate is awarded to dogs who show basic hunting skills.

The Irish Water Spaniel: A smart, strongly built sporting dog of great intelligence.

The Field Spaniel combines beauty and utility.

© Lara Suesens

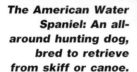

The American Water Spaniel: An all-around hunting dog, bred to retrieve from skiff or canoe.

Tracking

Spaniels have an excellent sense of smell. Indeed, English Springer Spaniels are often chosen by security forces as sniffer dogs, scenting out drugs, explosives, and other contraband.

In the competitive world, dogs are expected to track a human scent over a set course, which includes twists and turns, and then find an article at the end of it. Depending on the level—tracking dog, tracking dog excellent, variable surface tracking—the time elapsed since the course is set varies, and other degrees of difficulty are introduced, such as negotiating obstacles and increasing the number of articles to find.

Agility

This is a relatively recent sport—but it has taken the dog world by storm. Spaniels are bred to be working dogs, and they have no problem negotiating the obstacles around a course.

In competition, dogs are timed against the clock. Faults are given for missed contact points on the seesaw, A-frame, and dog walk and for poles down on the jumps. Dogs are eliminated for taking the wrong course.

Flyball

This sport is growing in popularity, and more and more breeds are trying it. Flyball is a relay race for dogs. The aim is for each dog to clear a series of hurdles, catch the ball from the flyball machine, and then speed back over the hurdles, ready for the next dog to go. The height of the hurdles depends on the size of the dogs on the

The American Cocker Spaniel: Merry and free, with a keen inclination to work.

The Clumber Spaniel: A long, low, heavy dog, with the power and endurance to move through dense undergrowth.

team. Spaniels have a strong instinct to retrieve and can pick up surprising speed over the hurdles. Flyball titles are awarded based on points that are accumulated.

Dog Shows

Dogs that are shown in the conformation ring must conform as closely as possible to the breed standard, which is the written blueprint for each breed. (Breed standards are featured in the chapters devoted to each breed.)

When the judge is deciding on rankings, it is the dog that he or she thinks comes closest to matching the breed standard that will gain the highest rank.

If you are interested in getting involved in the world of showing, you will need to train your

dog to perform in the show ring, which involves learning the show pose, gaiting (moving) correctly in the ring, and submitting to a hands-on examination by the judge.

Therapy Dogs

If you own a Spaniel, you are only too well aware of the wonderful companionship your dog gives to you and your family. Yet residents in homes for the elderly or patients in extended-care hospitals are deprived of this very special relationship.

There are now programs for taking dogs into institutions where they can visit the sick and the elderly. Such visits are hugely successful and have proved to be of enormous benefit. Many Spaniel breeds excel at this work.

CHAPTER TWO

CARING FOR YOUR SPANIEL

We are lucky that Spaniels are generally fit dogs, and with good care and management, most will go through life without suffering any major health problems. The most important first step is to buy a puppy from a reputable breeder. Obviously, you want to purchase a good-looking, typical representative of the breed you have chosen, but it is just as important to buy from a line that is as free as possible from inherited health conditions. A responsible breeder will have had all their breeding stock checked (e.g., hips x-rayed, eyes tested) before planning a mating, and the resulting puppies may also have health checks before they are sold (see page 22).

GETTING YOUR LINES RIGHT

Before you start looking for a breeder, ask yourself the following questions:

- Do you plan to work your Spaniel in the field?
- Do you want to exhibit your Spaniel in the show ring?
- Do you want to compete in one of the canine sports, such as agility or competitive obedience?
- Are you happy to have a family pet and have no plans to compete?

Breeders generally concentrate on working lines or show lines. Although there is a degree of crossover—some show kennels produce excellent working dogs and working kennels have produced champions in the show ring—it is better to take a specialist route.

Working Dogs

Spaniels produced from working lines tend to be high in energy and hunting drive. They may be lighter in build than the average show specimen, and depending on the breed, the coat may not be so luxurious. The breeder will have carried out some tests on the puppies (such as retrieving and noise tolerance) and will help you to pick a pup that has the makings of a good, working dog.

Show Dogs

If you have plans to show your Spaniel, you will obviously go to a show kennel. You must make your ambitions clear to the breeder so that the pups can be assessed with the breed standard in mind. The breeder will give you expert guidance, anxious that only the best representatives of the bloodlines go forward for exhibition. However, it is important to remember that you can pick a puppy with only show potential—there is no guarantee that the pup will develop into a show-quality adult.

Canine Sports

If you plan to compete with your Spaniel in one of the canine sports, you need to weigh the pros and cons of working and show lines and have a good look at the type of Spaniel that a particular breeder is producing. You want a dog that is motivated to work for you, but too strong a hunting drive could be a disadvantage.

American Water Spaniel: Some of the Spaniel breeds can be demanding in terms of training and exercise needs.

Companion Dogs

If are looking for a companion dog and have no ambitions to compete in the canine sports, you may find that a dog from working lines is a bit of a handful. Such dogs are bred to work long days in the field and will not be content with comparatively little physical exercise and mental stimulation. It is better to choose a Spaniel with a more laid-back temperament from a show kennel, which will fit in with your chosen lifestyle.

The breeder will know all the puppies in the litter and will help you to find the perfect pup. There is no doubt that you want a good-looking specimen, but you do not need to worry too much about the minor details. For example, if a pup has a great personality but its eyes are a shade too light according to the breed standard, it will not worry you one bit. However, if you are planning to show your dog, this may be a matter of considerable importance.

FINDING A BREEDER

There are a number of ways to locate breeders. You can use the Internet, log onto the American Kennel Club site (*www.akc.org*), and make use of the breeder referral service. The Kennel Club in the U.K. will put you in touch with breed club secretaries in your area who will have a list of reputable breeders. You can attend shows or working events, which will give you a chance to see lots of different dogs. This will give you a better knowledge of your chosen breed, and you will get an eye for the type of dog you like. You can then talk to the owners, who may have bred the dog, or they can put you in touch with the breeder. Many breeders also advertise in specialist dog magazines.

American Cocker Spaniels: Before you look for a breeder, decide what you want to do with your Spaniel.

© Jim Zimmerlin

Picking a Puppy

When you go to choose a puppy, you will be looking for specific breed features, such as color, but there are a number of points to consider that are applicable to all litters:

- Ideally, the puppies will be reared in a home environment, as this has proved to be valuable in early socialization. If this is not the case, check that the puppies have been handled frequently and brought into the house on a regular basis.
- The environment where the puppies are kept should be clean and fresh smelling.
- You should have the opportunity to see the mother with her puppies. Although she will not be looking her best after rearing a litter, she should appear fit and well and show evidence of a friendly nature.
- Arrange to see the puppies at a time when they are likely to be lively so that you can see them running around and playing. This will give you the chance to assess individual personalities.

- The puppies should be clean and plump—but obviously not too heavy for their size. Beware of pot-bellied puppies, as this is a sign of worm infestation.
- The puppies' coats should be clean with no sign of dandruff or skin irritation.
- There should be no discharge from either the eyes or the nose. The eyes should be bright and sparkling.
- Ears should be clean, with no bad odor.
- Check rear ends. Dirty or matted fur could be a sign of diarrhea.

FEEDING

The pet food industry is a multimillion dollar business, and there is a wide range of dog feeds available in a multitude of different forms and flavors. Obviously, the diet you choose is a matter of personal choice and convenience, and it may also depend on availability. However, it is important to bear in mind the following points:

- To begin with, stick to the diet the breeder has been using so that your pup does not have

Spaniels, like this English Springer, should be kept lean and healthy.

the trauma of adjusting to a new diet and a new home at the same time. It is often worth following the breeder's recommendations on diet, as he/she will have fed generations of dogs and will know what suits that particular breed.

- If you do need to change diet, do so gradually, adding increasing amounts of the new food at every meal over a period of days until the transition is complete.
- If you are feeding a complete diet, remember that it is complete: you do not need to add any supplements. In fact, adding supplements can be harmful, as this will upset the nutritional balance of the diet.
- If you are designing your own diet or using canned food, check the nutritional value of what you are feeding. It is vital that your dog is fed a good-quality diet that is correctly balanced.
- Feed according to age and lifestyle. The manufacturers of complete foods generally

have specially designed diets, such as junior, senior, lactating bitches, or working. If you are providing your own diet, bear the specific needs of your Spaniel in mind.
- Fresh drinking water should be freely available.

Obesity

When you see Spaniels in lean, working condition, what you have in front of you is a picture of health. Spaniels are meant to be active dogs—regardless of whether they are working—and it is vital that the correct weight is maintained. If a dog is allowed to become obese, the likelihood of serious health problems increases sharply. An overweight dog puts more strain on all its vital organs—particularly the heart—and life expectancy diminishes accordingly. Make sure your Spaniel does not become obese by observing the following guidelines:

- Match the quantity of food you are feeding to the amount of energy your Spaniel uses up.
- Never feed your Spaniel potato chips, chocolate, or any other human snack food.
- Do not feed treats between meals unless you are training. In this case, deduct the food you use as treats from your Spaniel's daily ration.
- When your Spaniel is full grown, take him to the vet to be weighed. If the vet is happy with your dog's weight, make a note of it. If you are concerned that your Spaniel is putting on weight, you will have a guideline to stick to.

ROUTINE CARE

You are responsible for your Spaniel's health and well-being, and so it is important that you keep

If plaque accumulates on the teeth, it will have to be removed with a tooth scaler.

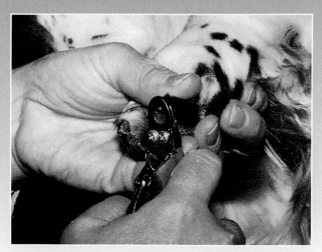

Ask your vet to show you how to trim nails.

a close check on him. Get into the habit of finding a time every week when you handle your Spaniel all over. This will mean that you spot any signs of trouble, such as lumps or bumps or skin irritations, at an early stage. In most cases, early diagnosis prevents a condition from becoming serious.

Each breed of Spaniel has its own grooming requirements (see the chapters devoted to the individual breeds), but there are a number of routine tasks that apply to all Spaniels.

Dental Care

The advent of complete diets, which are often fed moistened, means that most Spaniels do not keep their teeth clean naturally, as they would if they were eating hard biscuits, or chewing on bones.

Obviously you can provide your Spaniel with a marrow bone (or a dental chew), and he will certainly enjoy it. However, it is a good idea to plan a routine where you clean teeth twice or three times a week. This prevents tartar from accumulating on the teeth, and the gums can be kept clear of infection.

There is a range of doggy toothpastes that come in different meaty flavors, and you can apply the paste on a long-handled toothbrush or you may prefer to use a finger brush. If you introduce teeth cleaning at an early age, your Spaniel will soon get used to his weekly brushing.

Nails

Spaniels that are exercised regularly on hard surfaces will probably keep their nails short, but in most cases, routine trimming is required. If you are new to dog ownership, ask your vet to show you how to trim your Spaniel's nails. It is not a difficult task, but it is important that you do not cut into the quick of the nail, as this causes profuse bleeding. You can use guillotine nail clippers or if you are worried about clipping too much nail, you can use a nail file.

Ears

All Spaniels have long, pendulous ears of varying degree, which are more prone to infection than breeds with erect or semierect ears where fresh air can circulate more freely.

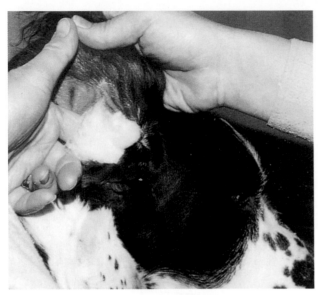

Spaniel ears need to be cleaned on a regular basis.

Make sure you check your Spaniel's ears on a weekly basis, and clean them if necessary. This can be done using a cotton ball and a cleanser recommended by your vet. Do not use cotton swabs, as you may probe too far into the ear canal and risk injury. It will help to keep the ears clean if you trim any hair growing on the inside. Take great care to ensure that hair does not fall into the ear canal.

If the inner ear is red and inflamed or foul smelling, you will need to seek veterinary advice. For information on ear mites and infections, see page 21.

PREVENTATIVE HEALTH CARE

There are a number of preventative health care measures you need to take to ensure your Spaniel stays fit and healthy. It is a good plan to keep a note in your diary as to when your dog has received various treatments and when the next are due so that you keep fully up-to-date.

Vaccinations

Your puppy will need to be vaccinated against the major infectious diseases that affect dogs. These include:

• Distemper
• Infectious hepatitis
• Parvovirus
• Leptospirosis
• Parainfluenza

Your vet will have his/her own policy as to what age to vaccinate, depending on the disease risk in the area. Generally, the first vaccination will be given from eight to 12 weeks, followed up by a second vaccination two weeks later. It was standard practice to give a booster vaccination every 12 months, but increasingly, vets are recommending that immunity levels be checked before giving a booster. Ask your vet for advice. In many countries, including the U.S., vaccination against rabies is also recommended. In this case, revaccination is advised every one to three years.

Internal Parasites

Dogs can be affected by a number of internal parasites, so deworming should be part of your routine health care. All puppies should follow a deworming program outlined by your vet. Once the dog is full grown, he will still need to be dewormed—but not so frequently. Again, follow a program recommended by your vet. Worms that may affect your dog include:

• Roundworm, which can be found in the alimentary tract and can cause significant damage in puppies.

- Tapeworm, which obtain their nutrients from the dog's intestine. More of a nuisance than a life-threatening parasite.
- Whipworm, most often picked up by dogs that have permanent access to grass runs. A heavy burden can cause diarrhea.
- Lungworm, there are a number of species of worms that affect the lungs. Affected dogs will cough, and if left untreated, the worm can cause considerable lung damage.
- Heartworm (common in North America), which can survive for up to five years living in the heart and produce microfilia that circulate in the blood. Ultimately leads to heart failure.
- Hookworm, the eggs or larvae can be swallowed, or the larvae can penetrate the skin and migrate through the tissues to the small intestine. Adult worms develop within two to three weeks; they suck blood and lay up to 20,000 eggs per day.

External Parasites

Regular routine treatment for the more common external parasites is an essential aspect of caring for your Spaniel. Fortunately, the products that are now available—spot-on applications, sprays, and tablets—are effective and easy to administer. Ask your vet for advice on the best product to use and the frequency of treatment.

The most common external parasites you will need to treat include the following:

- Fleas: These are very easy to pick up, and they spread with amazing speed. Both the dog and the environment should be treated on a routine basis. Allergies to fleas can result in skin irritations.

- Ticks: These are more likely to be picked up by dogs living in the country. The tick attaches itself to the host by its mouthpart, and care must be taken to remove the entire tick, including the mouthpart. Ticks are carriers of Lyme disease (which causes chronic arthritis). Although there is a preventative vaccine for dogs living in vulnerable areas of the United States, tick control is also important. Many products combine treatments for fleas and ticks.
- Ear mites attack the external ear and can be transmitted via close contact. The first signs are scratching and shaking the head. The dog may also have a brown discharge in the ear. Twice-daily cleaning is required plus treatment with medicated drops, prescribed by your vet.
- Harvest mites may affect Spaniels that are exercised in fields or woods during the autumn months. The mites live on decaying organic matter and, when picked up by a dog, cause intense irritation. Insecticidal sprays are the most effective form of treatment.

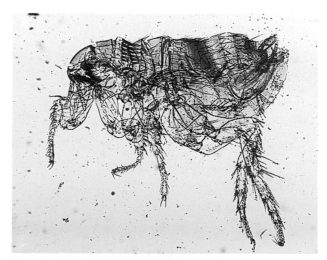

The dog flea—Ctenocephalides canis.

INHERITED CONDITIONS

There are a number of conditions that can be passed on from generation to generation, and all responsible breeders work hard at attempting to eliminate these potential problems from their lines. However, it is important to be aware of the conditions that may affect your chosen breed so that you can ensure that the appropriate checks have been carried out.

The most commonly inherited conditions that affect Spaniels include the following:

Hip Dysplasia

This is a malformation of the ball-and-socket joint of the hips, causing restricted movement and eventual arthritis. All breeding stock should be hip tested, and you should find out the average grade/score for your breed.

In the United States, hip testing is carried out by the Orthopedic Foundation for Animals (OFA). Hips are graded on a scale from 1–7 with Grade 1 being "excellent/normal" and Grade 7 being "severe dysplastic."

HIP DYSPLASIA RANKINGS		
Ranking	Breed	Registrations
5th	Clumber Spaniel	47.5
8th	Sussex Spaniel	41.9
40th	Field Spaniel	18.6
61st	English Springer Spaniel	14.3
63rd	Welsh Springer Spaniel	13.9
66th	Irish Water Spaniel	13.0
93rd	American Water Spaniel	8.3
101st	Cocker Spaniel (American)	6.3
111th	Cocker Spaniel (English)	5.7

In the U.K., a joint scheme is operated by the British Veterinary Association and the Kennel Club. Hips are scored on a points basis (each hip has a possible score of 53, and the total score is out of a possible 106). The higher score refers to the more dysplastic hip. Breed averages are published annually.

Since 1974, the OFA has collected data on breed incidence of hip dysplasia. It has worked out a ranking of breeds based on at least 100 evaluations. Those with a prevalence of more than 10 percent are considered to have hip dysplasia as a major concern, those with a prevalence of 5–10 percent have the condition as a minor concern.

For more information, visit the OFA web site at *www.offa.org*

Elbow Dysplasia

This term applies to any developmental disease of the elbow, usually resulting in arthritis.

Radiographic screening is carried out by the OFA when dogs are a minimum of two years old; the British scheme x-rays at 12 months of age. The grading is 0–3 with Grade 0 being "normal" and Grade 3 being "severe osteoarthritis."

The breeds most likely to be affected are the English Springer Spaniel (see page 71), the Welsh Springer Spaniel (see page 117), and the American Cocker Spaniel (see page 25).

Patellar Luxation

This is a dislocation of the knee joint, and it more commonly affects the Toy breeds and bow-legged breeds, such as the Staffordshire Bull Terrier. However, the American Cocker Spaniel is predisposed toward this condition (see page 25) and the English Springer Spaniel to a lesser extent. (see page 71).

Gastric Torsion
Often referred to as "bloat," this is when the stomach twists, trapping the contents and gasses. It is potentially fatal if left untreated. Large, deep-chested breeds are more commonly affected, but the American Cocker Spaniel is at risk (see page 25).

Congenital Heart Disease
Heart problems in Spaniels are few and far between. The only breed that is listed with a slight tendency is the American Water Spaniel (see page 37).

Epilepsy
This is a short-lasting but devastating disturbance of the nerve activity in the brain, which is expressed as fits or seizures. The cause may be liver or kidney disease, or there is a condition known as inherited or idiopathic epilepsy where the cause of the seizure is unknown. American Cocker Spaniels (see page 25) have been diagnosed with this inherited condition.

Deafness
Fortunately, this is rarely a problem in the Spaniel breeds, the only exception being parti-colored English Cocker Spaniels (see page 59). Testing is available for adults and puppies.

Eye Disorders
There are a number of eye disorders that may be inherited. Ask the breeder for incidence of the conditions in their bloodlines, and where

It is important to be aware of inherited conditions that could affect your Spaniel's health.

© D. Shields

relevant, check to see if eye tests have been carried out.

The most commonly inherited eye conditions in Spaniels include the following:

- **Entropion:** The eyelids turn inward, causing irritation and possible ulceration of the eye.
- **Ectropion:** The lower eyelids droop and turn outward, causing conjunctivitis.
- **Progressive retinal atrophy:** Retinal degeneration that causes night blindness, leading to total blindness. The condition makes its appearance between 12 and 30 months.
- **Glaucoma:** An increase of pressure in the eyeball, which can lead to sudden blindness.
- **Retinal dysplasia:** Occurs at birth. The retina is misshapen or detached. The condition can be diagnosed at six to seven weeks.
- **Cataracts:** Opacity/clouding of the lens, which has a varying effect on vision.

In North America, the Canine Eye Registration Foundation does invaluable work in testing adults and puppies and compiling data that can be used when selecting breeding stock.

CHAPTER THREE

THE AMERICAN COCKER SPANIEL

© Jim Zimmerlin

Loving, playful, bright as a button, and hugely glamorous, the American Cocker Spaniel has taken the dog world by storm and boasts a large and enthusiastic fan club.

Bred from the English Cocker Spaniel who was used for flushing woodcocks, the American Cocker specialized in flushing and retrieving quail—but it was not long before other qualities came to the fore. The smallest member of the Sporting/Gundog Group, the American Cocker is the ideal combination of sporting dog and lapdog. He is lively and energetic and can take part in all types of activities, but he is still small enough to pick up. He adores people, and having a cuddle with his beloved owner is his idea of bliss.

There is no doubt that the American Cocker is the most spectacular to look at of all the Spaniel breeds. Sturdy and compact in build, he has a rounded skull and a cleanly chiseled, refined head. His eyes are full and round, with a soft, appealing expression. The coat is flat and silky, with profuse feathering. The wonderful range of colors is a feature of the breed; they have been divided into three varieties: black, parti-color (which can include sable, roan, tricolor, and blue and white), and any solid color other than black (ASCOB) ranging from lightest cream to darkest red, including brown with tan points.

This is a breed that has had its fair share of controversy—purists say that the American Cocker is too far removed from its origins to be truly considered a Sporting Spaniel. In fact, the American Cocker is still valued as a hunting dog, and his docile nature makes him a willing worker. However, it is as a companion dog that the American Cocker really excels. His bubbly personality, his love of people, and his all-around adaptability means that he is a firm favorite in his native land and is growing in popularity worldwide.

BREED HISTORY

Although Spaniels are ancient in origin, the American Cocker Spaniel is a relatively recent innovation. The breed takes its origins from the

© Jim Zimmerlin

The most glamorous of the Spaniel breeds, the American Cocker has brains as well as beauty.

English Cocker Spaniel (see page 59). Obo II, an English import born around 1880, had a huge influence on the newly emerging Cocker Spaniel breed. It was not long before breeders were arguing over what the Cocker Spaniel should look like. Some American breeders wanted a smaller, low-set dog who would specialize in hunting quail and other small game. Increasingly, Cockers in England were becoming leggier, with a longer, stronger neck. For a number of years, imports and exports between the United States and England flourished, and the different varieties of Cocker Spaniel were often bred with each other.

It was the birth of Red Brucie, bred by Herman Mellenthin in the United States, that helped to clarify the situation. This dog was reckoned to be an excellent example of the American type, and he became the founding sire for the American Cocker.

Breed Recognition

Initially, English and American Cockers were considered as varieties of the same breed. At shows, the best American Cocker was judged against the best English Cocker, and the winner went through to compete in the Sporting Group.

The American variety was growing in popularity, and the English contingent was becoming worried that its type would be lost forever. In 1936, the English Cocker Spaniel Club of America was founded, and members campaigned vigorously for separate breed status. In 1946, the American Kennel Club finally granted their wish. From that time onward, the English Cocker and the American Cocker were registered as separate breeds, and both were entitled to go forward to compete in the Sporting Group. At the same time, all interbreeding between the two varieties was banned.

The Colors

The formal recognition of the American Cocker Spaniel resulted in a huge surge of popularity for the breed. At that time, the black Cocker was unbeatable in the show ring, and breeders applied for permission to show the new breed in three color varieties. The AKC agreed that the American Cocker could be exhibited as the black variety (which later included black and tans), parti-colors, and any solid color other than black (ASCOB).

Aficionados of the breed see distinct differences in temperament between the three varieties. Blacks tend to be the brightest, ASCOBs are more laid-back (except for chocolates, who seem to be a rule unto themselves), and parti-colors are sociable, excitable, and full of fun.

THE AMERICAN COCKER SPANIEL TODAY

Ranked as the 15th most popular breed in the United States, the American Cocker currently has annual registrations of 20,655. The English Cocker trails behind in 75th place. Predictably, the situation is reversed in the U.K., with the English Cocker rated the third most popular breed and the American Cocker listed in 65th position, with 549 registrations a year. To put this in context, the American Cocker is the third most popular of the nine Sporting Spaniel breeds in the U.K., which shows that it has gained considerable ground, particularly in recent years.

The Kennel Club in the U.K. and the American Kennel Club have drawn up their own very detailed standards for the breed, but they match closely in their descriptions of the ideal American Cocker. Interestingly, they both agree that feathering on the coat should not be so profuse as to affect performance as a sporting dog—but in reality, the glamorous, full-coated dogs that appear in the show ring would be incapable of working through undergrowth, let alone swimming to retrieve waterfowl.

General Appearance

A compact, sturdy dog with a refined head that is in complete balance with his body. He has strong, well-boned legs and stands well up at the shoulder.

Characteristics

Capable of speed combined with endurance, the American Cocker is merry and sound and shows a keen inclination to work.

The recognition of the American Cocker as a breed in its own right led to a huge surge in its popularity.

Temperament

Both the American and the British standards give very sparse descriptions compared with the detail given elsewhere, relying on, "Equable with no suggestion of timidity."

Head

The skull is well developed and rounded. The eyebrows are clearly defined, and there is a pronounced stop. The face, particularly around the eyes, is well chiseled, and the muzzle is broad, deep, and square with a well-developed nose. The nose is black in blacks, black and tans, and black and whites. In other colors, it is brown, liver, or black—the darker the better.

Eyes

The round, full eyes, looking directly forward,

The American Cocker is a compact, sturdy dog.

The refined head, with its rounded skull, is typical of the American Cocker. The expression is soft and appealing.

are a feature of the breed. The eye rims give a slightly almond-shaped appearance. The expression is intelligent, alert, soft, and appealing. The color of the iris is dark brown, and in general, the darker the better.

Ears

Long (extending to the nostrils), of fine leather, and set on no higher than the lower part of the eye. The ears are well clothed with long, silky, straight or wavy hair.

Mouth

Strong jaws with a perfect scissor bite (the upper teeth closely overlap the lower teeth).

Neck

Long enough to allow the nose to reach the ground easily, muscular, and free from throatiness. The neck rises strongly from the shoulders and arches slightly as it joins the head.

Forequarters

Deep, clean-cut shoulders, which are sloping without visible protrusion, and so set that the upper points of the withers are at an angle that permits a wide spring of rib. When viewed from the side, the elbow is directly below the highest point of the shoulder blade. The forelegs are straight, strongly boned, and muscular, set close to the body. The pasterns are short and strong.

Body

The height at the withers is approximately the same as the length of the body from the withers to the set-on of the tail. A deep chest, the lowest point no higher than the elbows and wide enough to allow for heart and lung space—but not so wide as to interfere with straightforward movement of the forelegs. Well-sprung ribs and a strong back that slopes slightly downward from the shoulders to the set-on of the tail.

Hindquarters

Wide hips and muscular, well-rounded quarters. The hind legs are strongly boned with moderate angulation at the stifle and powerful, clearly defined thighs. Hocks are strong and well let down. The hind legs should appear parallel when standing or moving.

Feet

Compact, round, and firm, with strong, tough pads.

Tail

Customarily docked by three-fifths, set on and carried on a line with the topline of the back or slightly higher but never straight up like a Terrier or so low as to indicate timidity. A merry action is typical of the breed.

Movement

Coordinated movement of the front and rear, smooth and effortless, covering the ground well.

Coat

Short and fine on the head, medium length on the body with enough undercoat to give protection. Feathering on the ears, chest, legs, and abdomen should not be so excessive as to hide the true lines and movement. The coat is silky, flat, or slightly wavy. Texture is most important—a curly, woollen, or cotton texture is undesirable.

Color

- *Black variety:* Solid jet black and black with tan points.
- *Any color other than black:* Any solid color ranging from lightest cream to darkest red, including brown and brown with tan points.

© Jim Zimmerlin

The American Cocker loves people and has a great sense of fun.

- *Parti-color:* Two or more solid or well-broken colors, one of which must be white. Roans are classified as parti-colors. Any of the above colors with tan points.
- *Tan points:* A clear spot above each eye, on the sides of the muzzle and under the cheeks, on the underside of the ears, on all feet and legs, under the tail, and optionally on the chest.

Size

Males 15 inches (37.5 cm) at the withers, females 14 inches (35 cm)—height may vary by half an inch above or below this ideal.

Disqualifications

These are confined to the American breed standard:

- *Height:* Males over 15.5 inches (38.75), females over 14.5 inches (36.25 cm).
- *Color and markings:* Only the colors described

in the standard are acceptable, any other colors or combination of colors to disqualify.

- *Black variety:* White markings except on chest and throat.
- *Any solid color other than black variety:* White markings except on chest and throat.
- *Parti-color variety:* Primary color 90 percent or more.
- *Tan points:* Tan markings in excess of 10 percent, absence of tan markings in black or ASCOB variety in any of the specified locations.

LIVING WITH AN AMERICAN COCKER SPANIEL

Beautiful to look at and fun to be with, the American Cocker quickly became established as a

Start training at an early age so you can build up a close bond with your American Cocker.

companion dog par excellence. However, the demand for the breed has led to overproduction, resulting in an increase in health problems and the emergence of untypical, unsound temperaments. It is essential to go to a breeder who has an impeccable reputation (see page 16) and to research bloodlines thoroughly so that you select an American Cocker that is sound in mind and body and is a credit to the breed.

Family Situation

The American Cocker is wholeheartedly a people dog, and he craves human companionship. He needs to be with his family—snuggled up on the sofa or joining in with whatever is going on—or he will be miserable.

An adaptable breed, the American Cocker is equally happy with town or country living, and he welcomes the company of other dogs, regardless of their size. He is tolerant of small animals, and many have formed close friendships with family cats. The American Cocker suits old or young people, but care should be taken that play with small children does not become too boisterous.

An energetic, excitable dog, the American Cocker alternates bursts of activity with periods of calm. He is an alert watchdog and will be quick to let you know when visitors are close by.

Trainability

The quick-witted American Cocker has a high level of intelligence, which he has demonstrated in many of the canine disciplines. Bred from sporting lines, this is a dog who has a will to work and who specializes in interacting closely with his handler. It is important to provide your

Cocker with mental stimulation, even if you do not wish to get involved in competition, or your dog will find mischief on his own.

Although small in size, the American Cocker is high on demand. He needs human company, he wants to be played with, he likes to use his brain, and he enjoys a cuddle. Owners need to satisfy these needs or else select a less-demanding breed. In fact, most owners find that fulfilling these needs is nothing but a pleasure.

Training should start at a young age, and handlers need to establish a sense of leadership. The American Cocker has a mind of his own. If he thinks he can get away with it, he will start to be in charge. For example, if an American Cocker decides he wants to sleep on the sofa and you sometimes let him, he will soon believe that he can sleep on the sofa whenever he likes and may even give a warning growl if you try to disturb him. In the same way, he may become possessive over toys or his food. You need to be confident and consistent in your handling so he understands his place in the family.

The American Cocker loves to perform, and it is well worth teaching him a repertoire of tricks so he can show off when friends come round.

Exercise

The American Cocker will be whatever you want him to be—an energetic dog who goes for long walks or a less-demanding companion who enjoys short excursions. The key is to provide a balance of mental and physical exercise so that your dog is fit and healthy and his mind is well occupied.

If you are not able to give your American Cocker a lot of exercise, make sure you provide varied and interesting outings. Do not neglect the value of play sessions, which will be fun for both you and your Cocker.

The feathering on an American Cocker is not intended to inhibit the dog's natural function. If you plan to take your dog on long country rambles or have access to a safe place to swim, though, you may consider trimming or clipping the coat so your dog can enjoy his exercise to the full.

Grooming

The long, silky coat of the American Cocker, in its spectacular range of colors, is one of the great attractions of the breed. However, owners need to be prepared to work hard to keep the coat in good order.

© Jim Zimmerlin

This is an energetic breed that thrives on exercise.

© Jim Zimmerlin

Dedicated grooming is required to keep the coat in good order.

Pet Grooming

- The silky coat tangles easily, so the American Cocker will need a grooming session two or three times a week. Use a pin brush, and work through the coat, going right down to the skin.
- A slicker brush can be used on the feathering, as its hooked steel pins help to break up the tangles. It may help to use a de-matter if the coat is tangled.
- Work through the coat again, using a comb with medium and fine teeth.
- If your American Cocker is neutered, the coat is inclined to become slightly cottony in texture, and this mats and tangles more easily.
- Clippers can be used on the head, face, neck, ears, and the topside of the paws, or you can trim these parts of the coat with scissors. The hair between the toes and under the tail will also need to be trimmed.

- If you are working your American Cocker in the field or you do not want to get involved in lengthy grooming sessions, you can keep him in a low-maintenance pet or utility clip.

Show Grooming

- Clippers cannot be used on a show dog, as they spoil the texture of the coat. This means that the coat needs to be groomed on a daily basis, and the hair is stripped out using finger and thumb or a stripping knife. Bathing and trimming is needed every two weeks.

Health Concerns

Responsible breeders are striving to eliminate inherited conditions from the breed, but you may need to address the following issues.

- **Glaucoma:** This is a major concern in the breed (see page 23).
- **Cataracts:** This is another significant condition in the breed (see page 23).
- **Progressive retinal atrophy:** This is not a widespread problem, but breeding stock should be eye tested (see page 23).
- **Patellar luxation:** The American Cocker is ranked third in the OFA's listing of breed incidence for this condition. Out of a total of 274 evaluations, 70.8 were normal, and 29.2 were affected.
- **Hip dysplasia:** Ranked 101st in the OFA's listing, 6.3 percent of dogs that were tested proved to be affected.
- **Skin conditions:** Lipfold pyoderma, otitis externa, and seborrhea crop up in the breed.
- **Kidney conditions:** Familial renal disease and congenital hypoplasia affect kidney growth and shorten life expectancy.

- **Epilepsy:** A minor concern in the breed.
- **Canine rage syndrome:** This is a condition where a normally placid dog inexplicably attacks and later seems unaware of his behavior. It is a rare condition, and research is currently being carried out to find possible causes and effective treatments.

NEW CHALLENGES

The American Cocker Spaniel should not be underestimated. He is bright and loves to show off—and you can guarantee that he will turn heads in whatever sport he competes in.

Hunting

There are advocates for taking the American Cocker Spaniel out of the Sporting Group because he has become more of a glamorous show dog, but field enthusiasts claim the American Cocker has retained his sporting instincts. A specialist bird dog, the American Cocker quarters the ground at a fast, snappy pace but approaches his quarry, which is often well hidden, at a slower pace, giving a soft flush. He will retrieve from land and also from water.

Obedience

Highly trainable, the American Cocker has proved successful in competitive obedience, although owners who take up the challenge are relatively few and far between.

Agility

Many owners comment on their dogs' love of jumping, and so agility is a natural choice for the American Cocker and suits his exuberant nature.

A specialist bird dog, the American Cocker is valued in the field for its soft flush and its reliable retrieve.

The American Cocker is quick-witted and fast, which is an ideal combination for agility.

© Jim Zimmerlin

A natural showman, the American Cocker excels at canine freestyle.

Tracking

Like all sporting Spaniels, the American Cocker has natural scenting abilities, which can be put to good use.

Showing

Keeping an American Cocker in full show coat is extremely labor intensive—but there is no more glamorous sight than an American Cocker in full flow as he gaits effortlessly around the show ring.

Canine Freestyle

This discipline is perfectly suited to the American Cocker's flamboyant style. If you have the dedication to work at the complex movements required, you will create a winning partnership.

Therapy Dogs

The perfect, typical temperament of the American Cocker is loving and affectionate, and those that become involved in therapy work are true ambassadors for the breed.

COCKER CRAZY

Larry and Mary Joan Kunkle and their daughter, Shannon McCracken, are devoted American Cocker Spaniel fans, breeding and showing their dogs as a family.

Joan says, "When I was a child, I adopted a stray dog, who I called Petey. I think he had some Cocker in him and we were devoted to each other. Some years later, as a married woman with children of my own, I was given a parti-colored male Cocker puppy. We named him Barrel Valley Magic Bandit, the Barrel Valley coming from the name of the valley where we live, which has now become our kennel name. We called him Magic for short. Magic had all the qualities that endear the Cocker to people worldwide—the appealing eyes, merry personality, boundless energy, and just the right size to fill your lap. After that, we were hooked on Cockers."

Shannon agrees. "After Magic, it was easy to love the whole breed," she says. "The second and third additions to our family came easily. Cockers are small, and they adapt to almost any setting, from a small apartment to a country farm, and they are great with children. I remember Magic being on my heels everywhere I went as a child, and we got into just about as much mischief as we could manage. Magic's soulful eyes begging for forgiveness were great for getting us both out of trouble!"

The family's love of Cockers soon took them into the world of conformation shows. A friend showed Cairn Terriers, and she offered to give informal handling lessons to Shannon, who began competing in some local puppy matches. It wasn't long before she entered her first all-breed show. Shannon recalls, "Mom told everyone that she did it to keep me busy and out of trouble. If so, it certainly worked. Showing is wonderful but it is all-consuming. Now, my non-dog friends think I'm crazy to put so much effort into something that doesn't make money, but it's not about money."

Shannon and her parents learned about conformation shows slowly, starting at the bottom and working their way up. Joan recalls, "It took a long time to learn how to show a dog properly, to present its best qualities. To win in the conformation ring takes a lot of hard work and determination. It's not a sport for the faint-hearted. Even in those early days when we lost, however, we learned some valuable lessons." Shannon learned to lose graciously as, in later days, she learned to win graciously.

"Shannon's very first show took place on a

Shannon, aged eight, showing Lady Catrin of Barval (Kitty).

bitterly cold October day, at a sanctioned puppy match. The dog she entered with—Kitty (Lady Catrin of Barval)—was not really show quality, but we didn't really know that at the time. We didn't have a clue about the finer points of trimming, but to us Kitty looked beautiful, freshly bathed and clipped. When the judge chose Kitty for first place that day, we were all bitten by the showing bug—although we lost a lot in those early days."

Shannon recalls, "Because I started off as a child among the adults, I made many mistakes. Most of them were very amusing to spectators. Having figured out the finer points of showing, I thought it might be cute to teach the dogs some extra tricks to show off in the ring, so I taught one of our dogs, Cajun, how to lie down and play dead. I realized my mistake the first time a judge pointed at Cajun and he promptly keeled over!

Continued on page 36

Continued from page 35

"Most important is a willingness to learn. Cockers are not the easiest breed to compete with. Professional handlers are common because of the high-maintenance coat, which requires a great deal of work to keep it in top condition. It's hard to compete at the top level. To compete against them, you need a quality dog, who must be trained, groomed, and conditioned to the highest level. Then you must learn to present your dog as well as—or better than—the professionals."

For the Barrel Valley clan, their success in the ring really began to improve as a result of Joan's interest in genetics, which began when she was in high school. Joan says, "Slowly, we improved our Cockers and eventually bred our first conformation champion, Riggs (Ch. Barrel Valley Lethal Weapon). It certainly improved our prospects in the show ring, but I wouldn't advise anyone else interested in taking up showing their own home-bred dogs to follow the route my family and I have. Instead, you should find a mentor, someone long established and highly knowledgeable about the breed. Learn everything you can from them and about your breed before you even think about purchasing a foundation dog. Then buy the very best you can. Start with the best, then breed to the best, but be sure you know what the best is before you start."

Joan takes breeding very seriously, commenting that "For many years, the Cocker Spaniel was the most popular dog in the U.S., to the detriment of the breed. Irresponsible breeding caused a decline in health and temperament. We like to think that Barrel Valley Cockers are helping to change that, producing dogs that are as sound in health and temperament as they are in physical beauty. Cockers should be more than just a pretty face; they should live long and healthy lives with their families."

In 2003, Tommy (Ch. Barrel Valley Ransom) was named as one of the top-ten producers of champions in the United States, with four of his sons and daughters finishing their championships owner handled. Joan and Shannon agree that it is one of their most proud moments, not only to see the fantastic results from Joan's carefully planned breeding program but also because Shannon has shown that she can compete with the best professional handlers around.

Joan sums up her love for Cockers and the conformation ring by saying, "The Cocker, being the smallest member of the Sporting Group, has all the attributes of a sporting dog in a package small enough to fit any household. The Cocker can do it all and is happy to do so." Shannon concurs, "The Cocker can do it all, anywhere and with anyone."

Barrel Valley Buzz Bombe: Barrel Valley's first group-placing dog.

CHAPTER FOUR

THE AMERICAN WATER SPANIEL

The little brown dog from America—the American Water Spaniel—is one of about ten breeds that originated in the United States. Surprisingly, he remains something of a secret. Despite his outstanding working abilities, he is little known outside his native home and is rarely seen in the show ring. The breed is recognized in the U.S. and Canada and by the Federation Cynologique Internationale (FCI), but there are no registrations with the Kennel Club in England.

Bred to be a cold-water retriever, the American Water Spaniel's job was to travel in a skiff or canoe with his owner and then leap from the side into icy waters to retrieve shot geese or duck. A keen hunter, the versatile American Water Spaniel was also used to track and retrieve prairie chicken, ruffed grouse, and rabbit. In the early days of the breed, these hardworking hunters were also expected to protect the home and family.

Loyal and docile, the American Water Spaniel tends to bond closely with his family and usually focuses his attention on one individual. Although a friendly type, he has a tough and determined side to his character. This is a breed that knows his own mind and needs an experienced owner.

To look at, the American Water Spaniel is very much a working dog rather than a glamorous show dog. He is solidly built and muscular but fairly small in size, measuring 15–18 inches (38–45.5 cm) at the shoulder. The tail is not docked as it performs an important function, acting as a rudder when the dog is swimming. The head is framed by long, wide ears, and the typical expression is one of self-confidence and intelligence. The American Water Spaniel was expected to swim in cold waters and to hunt in marshland and through thickets of bramble. So he has the coat to deal with these demanding conditions. The undercoat is dense, and the top coat is tightly curled or falls in uniform waves. The color is solid liver, brown, or chocolate.

Sometimes known as the "poor man's dog" because the breed was small and cheap to feed,

the American Water Spaniel remains a specialist sportsman's dog and has also proved his worth as an affectionate and lively companion dog.

BREED HISTORY

The first records of a cold-water retrieving dog come from the American Midwest in the 1800s. At that time, hunters in Wolf and Fox River Valley regions of Wisconsin had a tough life, hunting waterfowl and trapping game. They needed a small, all-around dog who could flush and retrieve all types of game. For the most part, the hunters worked from skiffs. So a dog who was light enough to get on and off the small boats and could swim and retrieve shot or wounded birds was essential. In addition, the huntsmen wanted to take advantage of rabbits and other game on land. So the dog had to double as a land dog, tracking hidden quarry, flushing it out for the gun, and then retrieving it.

It is thought that a number of breeds were used to develop this versatile hunting dog. The ancient English Water Spaniel, which later became extinct, was crossed with the Irish Water Spaniel, which was brought to America by Irish immigrants. The Curly Coated Retriever and the Sussex Spaniel were also used to create this all-American sporting dog.

In the early days, the dog's working ability was of paramount importance. Apart from maintaining size (generally around 40 pounds/ 18 kg) and color, there was little interest in developing a uniformity of type that would result in a recognizable breed. These dogs were known variously as the Brown Water Spaniel or simply as Browns or Brownies.

Founding Father

By the late 19th century, the American Water Spaniel was losing its place as the chosen dog of hunters in the Midwest. As more breeds were recognized, there was increasing specialization as dogs were called on to perform specific tasks. The Labrador Retriever and the Golden Retriever were used as water retrievers, Setters and Pointers were used on open land, and the flushing Spaniels, particularly the English Springer Spaniel, became expert at working in cover.

The American Water Spaniel may well have died out but for the efforts of one man, Dr. Fred J. Pfeiffer of New London, Wisconsin. He was a passionate hunter and always worked with American Water Spaniels. He established the Wolf River Kennels and developed his own breeding program. At any one time, he would have more than 100 dogs in his kennel.

The American Water Spaniel is highly prized as a cold-water retriever. © Lara Suesens

The American Water Spaniel is a top-class hunting dog with a small but devoted following.

However, it was not enough that he had created a stronghold for the breed, he was determined to get official recognition so that the future of the American Water Spaniel would be assured.

Dr. Pfeiffer campaigned tirelessly and succeeded in founding a breed club and formulating a breed standard, which was essential in establishing uniformity of type. The breakthrough came in 1920 when the United Kennel Club (the second largest registry for purebreds) gave official recognition to the American Water Spaniel, followed by the American Kennel Club in 1940.

THE AMERICAN WATER SPANIEL TODAY

This is a breed that has a small but dedicated following. The current American Kennel Club data ranks the American Water Spaniel 120th, with annual registrations of 196. Why is it that this top-class hunting dog, who is handy in size and easy to keep, failed to reach the popular heights of the other breeds created in the United States?

The American Water Spaniel's workmanlike appearance may go against him in the show ring, although there is no doubt that the breed has its own special charm. A far more likely reason for the breed's low numbers is that the AKC does not classify the breed as either a Spaniel or a Retriever. This means that American Water Spaniels cannot compete in AKC hunting tests or field trials. A number of dedicated breeders, who believe the breed should be classified as a Spaniel, are trying to change this situation. In 1993, they formed the American Water Spaniel Field Association, which is campaigning for the AKC to reconsider its position. The association also organizes field training sessions and other events exclusively for the American Water Spaniel.

Breeders adhere to the AKC breed standard. Because the American Water Spaniel has never become fashionable, there have been very few changes in his appearance since the earliest days.

General Appearance
An all-around hunting dog, the American Water Spaniel is medium sized, active, and muscular. He is solidly built; full of substance, strength and quality; and should never appear clumsy. The curly or marcel (uniform waves) coat is a feature of the breed.

Breed Characteristics
The correct size is an essential of the breed, which was used to retrieve from skiff or canoe and work ground with relative ease. He is

slightly longer than tall, but exact proportions are not as important as the dog being well balanced and capable of performing his intended function.

Temperament

Great eagerness and energy for the hunt are typical of the American Water Spaniel, but he should still be controllable in the field. He is intelligent, eager to please, and friendly.

Head

This must be in proportion to the overall dog. The skull is rather broad and full, and the stop is moderately defined. The muzzle is moderate in length, with good depth. The nose is wide with well-developed nostrils to ensure good scenting power.

Eyes

Medium-sized eyes are set well apart. They are slightly rounded and should not appear bulging. The color can range from light yellowish brown to brown, hazel, or of dark tone to harmonize with the coat. A dog with yellow eyes is disqualified from the show ring. The breed standard makes the point that yellow refers to a bright color—like that of a lemon—and should not be confused with light yellowish brown. The American Water Spaniel has an attractive expression, which shows alertness, self-confidence, and intelligence.

Ears

Set on slightly above the eye line but not too high on the head. The ears are long and wide and should extend to the nose.

A solidly built dog of substance and strength.

Mouth

The lips are clean and tight, without excess skin or flews. The teeth should meet in a scissor bite (upper teeth closely overlapping the lower teeth) or a level bite (the front teeth on the upper and lower jaws meet exactly, edge to edge).

Neck

The neck is round and muscular. It is of medium length and is free from throatiness. The American Water Spaniel's neck should not be arched, but he should carry his head with dignity.

Forequarters

The sloping shoulders are clean and muscular. The legs are of medium length; they are straight and well boned but not so short as to handicap work in the field or so heavy as to appear clumsy. The pasterns are strong.

Body

Well developed and sturdily constructed but not too compactly coupled. The brisket is well

The skull is broad, and the ears are set slightly above the eye line.   © Lara Suesens

developed, extending to the elbows, and should not be too broad or too narrow. The ribs are well sprung, and the loins are strong.

Hindquarters

Well-developed hips and thighs with the rear assembly showing strength and drive. The hock joint is slightly rounded, and the length of leg from hocks to footpad is moderate. Hocks are parallel.

Feet

The size of the feet should harmonize with the size of the dog. The toes are closely grouped, webbed, and well padded.

Tail

Of moderate length and curved in a rocker fashion, the tail can be carried either slightly below or above the level of the back. It is tapered and has moderate feathering. It is lively in action.

Movement

The American Water Spaniel moves with well-balanced reach and drive. When viewed from the front, there should be no sign of the elbows being out. When viewed from the rear, the muscled hind legs should move as nearly parallel as possible, with the hocks flexing well, giving an appearance of power and strength.

Coat

The coat can range from marcel (uniform waves) to tightly curled. The amount of waves or curls can vary from one area to another on the dog. There should be sufficient density of undercoat to provide protection against weather, water, or punishing cover. The ears are well covered with hair on both sides, and the tail and the legs are moderately feathered. The forehead is covered with short, smooth hair without a topknot.

Color

Solid liver, brown, or dark chocolate. A little white on the toes and chest is permissible.

Size

Males and females are both 15–18 inches (38–45.5 cm) at the shoulder.

Weight: Males 30–45 pounds (13.6–20.4 kg), females 25–40 pounds (11.3–18.2 kg).

LIVING WITH AN AMERICAN WATER SPANIEL

Tough, active, and intelligent, the virtues of the American Water Spaniel, beyond his prowess as a hunting dog, are largely underrated. This is an easy breed to care for. In the right hands, he is a first-rate companion.

You may have to wait a while until puppies are available.   © Lara Suesens

Family Situation

In terms of size, the American Water Spaniel can adapt to urban living. In this situation, though, he needs to be given extensive exercise or he will be bored and may develop deviant behavior.

This is a breed that bonds strongly with one person, and so care should be taken if he is living in a family situation. He is naturally friendly and good-natured and will get on well with children as long as a strong sense of mutual respect is established.

The American Water Spaniel is generally tolerant of other dogs, and he certainly prefers his own kind. In the days of big hunting kennels, the dogs were kept very much as a pack. If you have more than one American Water Spaniel, you will need to be careful that the dogs do not bond so closely with each other that they have no time for you.

The breed was traditionally used as a watchdog and protector of the home, and most American Water Spaniels will be quick to give a vocal warning if strangers are approaching. Some owners report that the American Water Spaniel yodels when he is in full cry.

Trainability

The American Water Spaniel has a strong work ethic, and this will need to be channeled if he is not being used as a hunting dog. Prospective owners should think seriously about the amount of time they can give to training and the need for mental stimulation before choosing the breed.

The American Water Spaniel is slow to mature, and this means that a certain degree of patience is needed to allow the dog to grow up. Early socialization is particularly important so that your dog learns to accept all types of situations.

Watch out for any dominant tendencies as this is a breed that can question its status in the family. However, the American Water

This is a breed with a very strong work ethic.

Rain, shine—or snowing—the American Water Spaniel is always ready for exercise. © Lara Suesens

Spaniel is keen to find a focus for his devotion. As long as he finds someone to respect, he will be content to accept the house rules that are laid down.

Although the American Water Spaniel has a natural tendency to focus on one person, make sure this does not get out of hand. It is fine if the dog will work for only one owner, but he should be ready to accept directions from all members of the family. It will help if the dog is allowed to meet lots of different people. Then he will be more inclined to be sociable rather than being protective of his special person.

Exercise

This is a dog that was bred to be both tough and tireless. As a result, he needs outlets for his energy.

In the heyday of the breed, teams of dogs worked all day, repeatedly diving into freezing-cold water to retrieve shot or wounded game. The American Water Spaniel is superbly adapted to swimming. He has webbed feet, and he uses his tail like a rudder to help him change direction. If you have access to a safe stretch of water, you can play retrieve games and enjoy watching the breed at its very best. If you stay long enough, your dog may even get tired!

On land, the American Water Spaniel has a powerful sense of smell and is used to working in heavy cover. He will therefore relish the opportunity to enjoy a long ramble where he can go on the trail of exciting scents.

If you live in the city, be prepared to give your dog at least three periods of exercise a day. If possible, also get involved in a training activity (see below), which will provide mental and physical exercise.

Grooming

The weatherproof, waterproof, brambleproof coat is a feature of the breed, but despite its amazing protective qualities, it is easy to care for. There is a distinct oiliness to the texture of the coat, which helps to repel water. This can make an American Water Spaniel smell a bit "doggy." If his skin is clean and his coat is groomed, this is only a minor consideration.

- The coat will need to be brushed thoroughly once a week using a pin or bristle brush.
- A slicker brush can be used on the feathering, making sure the hair is free of mats and tangles.
- The ears need special attention as they have hair growing on both sides.
- Excess hair at the ear canal should be trimmed to prevent ear infections.
- Hair that grows between the pads will also need routine trimming.

- The breed standard states, "Coat may be trimmed to present a well-groomed appearance; the ears may be shaved; but neither is required." In most cases, show ring exhibitors will tidy up the feathering on the ears, legs, tail, and underside and will also ensure that the hair on the top of the head is smooth.
- Some hunters keep the coat trimmed all the way down in order to overcome the problem of burrs.

Health Concerns

This active, working dog is built on strong, simple lines and suffers from few major health problems. Check out the following:

- **Cataracts:** These do occur, and breeding stock should be eye tested (see page 23).
- **Progressive retinal atrophy:** A minor concern, but check out the bloodlines of preceding generations (see page 23).
- **Hip dysplasia:** The American Water Spaniel is listed 93rd by the OFA, with 8.3 percent of dogs tested diagnosed with the condition.
- **Congenital cardiac disease:** The American Water Spaniel is listed 9th in terms of incidence of cardiac disease. A study evaluating 105 dogs found 96.2 percent normal, 2.8 percent equivocal, and 1 percent affected.

NEW CHALLENGES

Highly intelligent and easy to motivate, the American Water Spaniel has the ability to excel in most of the canine sports. Scarcity of numbers means that he rarely has the opportunity to make his mark.

© Lara Suesens

Highly prized by sportsmen, the American Water Spaniel makes an excellent hunting companion.

Hunting

The American Water Spaniel is still highly prized by sportsmen. A strong and fearless swimmer, he excels as a water retriever, but he also works well close to the gun. Sportsmen remark that four or five birds will be shot, and the American Water Spaniel will mark each bird and retrieve them all in turn. In the field, a close affinity with his handler is of great benefit as he is easy to control. The current problem over classification (see page 40) is an obstacle to the breed achieving wider recognition for its superb hunting ability.

Agility

The American Water Spaniel is built more for strength and stamina than pure speed, but he has the energy and the enthusiasm to tackle all the obstacles on an agility course.

A highly intelligent dog, the American Water Spaniel will enjoy the challenge of obedience exercises.
© Lara Suesens

Obedience

A natural choice for competitive obedience, the American Water Spaniel has no problem in mastering the exercises, and he loves to work closely with his owner.

Flyball

The first American Water Spaniel has been awarded a flyball championship title. So clearly this is a sport where the breed can reach the top level.

Tracking

Like many of the Spaniel breeds, the American Water Spaniel has an excellent sense of smell.

He also has the persistence to follow a trail, even when it is over challenging terrain.

Showing

Although the American Water Spaniel is not numerically strong in the show ring, it can be boasted that the breed remains truly dual purpose. A show dog would be perfectly capable of working in the field, and vice versa.

Therapy Dogs

An even-tempered and affectionate dog, the American Water Spaniel's wonderful temperament means that he would be an asset to this type of work.

A HUNTER'S TALE

Linda Ford, from California, participates in hunting tests with her American Water Spaniels. She has been involved with four of her dogs—12-year-old Max (SR California Maximilian CDX, CGC, WD), nine-year-old Katie (SR California Katie Belle, CD, WD), six-year-old Star (SR CH California Star Attraction CD, WD), and six-year-old Joy (SR CH Kei-Rins California Joy CD, WD, CGC). She is now training three more for hunt tests later in the year.

"I first came across American Water Spaniels when researching different breeds for a friend of mine. He hunted ducks and wished he could find a smaller breed than the Labradors or Chesapeake Bay Retrievers that most of his friends had. After being around an American Water Spaniel for a while, I quickly fell in love with the breed. It wasn't long before I began to breed them myself and I have now established a good kennel—California American Water Spaniels.

"Hunting tests combine two great passions of mine—dogs and hunting. I have always been surrounded by friends who hunt with their dogs, and I decided to become involved with training my own dogs for hunting. I joined some clubs and started training my dogs for the field. I found that competing in hunt tests regularly helped me to stay focused on training and it was also a great deal of fun! I'd advise anyone taking it up to join a club with people who are already familiar with running hunt tests. I found that their input and help during training was invaluable.

"Hunt tests are supposed to resemble real hunting situations. So, depending on the type of hunt test and the level you are working, your dog must find and flush game, retrieve game from land and water, and work with multiple marks. It is quite challenging but very rewarding. It is vital that you are able to control your dog in the field. Obedience is a must! If you don't put that effort in, you can be left feeling quite embarrassed. For example, if you wing a bird and it hits the ground running and if you haven't done that extra obedience work for control, your dog and the bird will be out of gun range and you'll have a hard time getting the dog back so that you can continue with your hunting!

"American Water Spaniels were bred to work in the field, and, as a breeder, it gives me a great deal of pleasure to see the breed fulfilling its natural instinct to hunt and find game. You can clearly see the joy that the dog experiences when working and the pride he feels when he returns to you with the bird.

"One of the best moments I get is when I take out one of my puppies to work his first day in the field. He is so proud when he brings that bird in to you. As a breeder of American Water Spaniels, I am very concerned about producing dogs that perform well in the field and giving all my dogs the chance to experience the thrill of what they were originally bred for."

Breeder Linda Ford loves to see her dogs work.

CHAPTER FIVE

THE CLUMBER SPANIEL

Sedate, stoical, and big-hearted, the Clumber Spaniel has tremendous virtues—but in many ways, he is the odd one out of the Sporting Spaniels. He is a heavy dog, and his pace is leisurely. He thinks before he acts, and although he has the stamina to work all day in the field, he is not an energetic type.

However, in common with other Spaniel breeds, the Clumber loves his family. He is sweet tempered and affectionate and will reward his owners with steady devotion. A typical Clumber will spend the day napping and then have a sudden burst of exuberance. He will wag his whole back end in greeting and will curve himself into a "U" shape as he comes sidling up. The chances are he will have something in his mouth. Most of the Spaniel breeds love to carry toys, but the Clumber has a passion for it. He will pick up anything he can find and will often hoard toys in his bed.

The Clumber may appear slightly more aloof than the other Spaniel breeds and may initially be reserved with strangers.

A highly intelligent dog, the Clumber works closely with his handler. In a hunting situation, he will often wait for his owner to catch up with him, which makes him the preferred choice of older sportsmen. The Clumber's sense of smell is legendary and is said to be second only to a Basset Hound.

The Clumber Spaniel is a heavy-boned dog who gives an impression of strength. He is long and low to the ground, with a deep chest and powerful hindquarters. His head is massive, and his amber eyes have a pensive expression. The gleaming white coat is a feature of the breed, with lemon or orange head markings.

A steady and reliable worker in the field, the Clumber Spaniel's greatest claim to fame is his impeccable temperament. Once you have owned a Clumber, no other breed will do.

BREED HISTORY

Just as the Clumber Spaniel looks different from the other Spaniel breeds, he also has a very different history. It is thought that the ancestors of the breed came from France. The Alpine Spaniel appears to have played an important part in the development of the Clumber, and some historians believe that the Basset Hound was also used to give the Clumber his long, low-set body.

The duc de Noailles was a keen sportsman, and he started his own kennel of dogs, which he bred for many generations. They were big, heavy-set dogs with an outstanding sense of smell. With the onset of the French Revolution, the duc was fearful that his home would be lost. He applied to the Duke of Newcastle and asked him to provide a sanctuary for his dogs on his estate—Clumber Park in Nottinghamshire. The

The Clumber Spaniel was bred to retrieve from dense undergrowth, but is equally at home in the water.   © Abbyford Clumber Spaniels

dogs were moved, and the duke named them after his country seat.

The Duke of Newcastle was delighted with his new dogs and immediately started his own breeding program. Interestingly, there is an early visual record of the breed in England in a painting called *The Return From Shooting* by Francis Wheatley. Painted in 1788, it shows the second Duke of Newcastle with three of his Clumber Spaniels, who look remarkably like the dogs of today.

Noble Connections

The Clumber Spaniel's specialty as a hunting dog was to work in dense undergrowth. He worked slowly and diligently, and his keen nose led him to find and flush out game in almost impenetrable thickets. He retrieved to hand, proved to be a surprisingly good swimmer, and was ready to swim considerable distances to retrieve shot birds.

The Duke of Newcastle was keen to show off his dogs to other members of the nobility. Prince Albert, consort of Queen Victoria, was highly impressed and took a special interest in the breed. Earl Spencer, the Duke of Portland, and Lord Arthur Cecil all took dogs from Clumber Park and started their own breeding programs. The breed received wider recognition when Edward VII started his own strain of Clumber Spaniel, which he bred under the Sandringham prefix.

Determined to keep the breed pure, the nobility was careful to ensure that Clumber Spaniels did not get into the hands of the commoners. As a result, the breed was little known outside the great shooting estates.

Official Recognition

Clumber Spaniels were one of the first breeds to be shown in England, making their show ring debut in 1859. This led to wider recognition of the breed, and dog fanciers were quick to see the virtues of this impressive-looking dog who stood out so distinctly from the other Spaniel breeds.

In 1884, the first Clumber Spaniel reached North America, courtesy of Lieutenant Venables of Her Majesty's 97th Regiment, stationed in Halifax, Nova Scotia. They were eventually introduced to the United States, and the first Clumber Spaniels were registered in 1878. They became one of the first 10 breeds to be recognized by the American Kennel Club in 1884.

THE CLUMBER SPANIEL TODAY

The Clumber Spaniel has never reached the dizzy heights of top popularity. This has been of benefit to the breed, which remains very true to the original type. In the United States, the Clumber Spaniel is currently ranked 121st in breed listing, with annual registrations of 188. In the U.K., it is ranked at number 113, with 134 registrations a year.

The modern Clumber Spaniel retains a strong hunting instinct and is more than capable of withstanding the rigors of working in the field. His temperament is outstanding, and he is highly valued as a companion as well as an impressive show dog. For a breed that is relatively small in numbers, the Clumber can boast two major honors. In 1991 Sh. Ch. Raycroft Socialite won the prestigious Best In Show award at Crufts, and in 1996, Ch. Clussexx Country Sunrise took honors at the U.S.'s top event, the Westminster Dog Show.

Crufts Best in Show winner Sh. Ch. Raycroft Socialite, pictured with owner Ralph Dunne.

Over the last 50 years, the breed has become noticeably heavier, and a number of specimens are top weight or even heavier. It is important that breeders do not sacrifice the breed's soundness and working ability in pursuit of producing a dog of great substance.

Here is a picture in words of what the ideal Clumber Spaniel should look like, based on the British and American breed standards:

General Appearance

A long, low, heavy-boned dog, who gives the impression of strength, power, and endurance, he has massive bone and a heavy brow, with a typically thoughtful expression.

Breed Characteristics

The Clumber has a dignified stature that complements his stoical nature. A determined worker, he works silently and diligently using his excellent nose.

Temperament

Steady, kind, and reliable, the Clumber Spaniel is loyal and affectionate. He may be slightly reserved with strangers.

Ch. Clussexx Country Sunrise wins the big one—
Best in Show at Westminster Kennel Club.

Head

The head is termed "massive." It is square and of medium length. The top of the skull is broad, with a pronounced occiput. The brows are heavy, and there is a deep stop. The flews are well developed; the nose is large and square and colored shades of brown. The head should be free from exaggeration.

Eyes

Dark amber in color with a soft expression, slightly sunk, and showing some haw. Light eyes are highly undesirable.

Ears

Large and vine shaped, with a rounded lower edge, they are attached to the skull at eye level and hang slightly forward. They are covered with straight hair; the feathering should not extend below the ear leather.

Mouth

The jaws are strong, and the teeth should meet in a scissor bite (the upper teeth closely overlapping the lower teeth and set close to the jaw).

Neck

A fairly long neck that is thick and muscular, fitting into well-laid-back shoulders.

Forequarters

The shoulders are strong, sloping, and muscular. The forelegs are short, straight, and heavy in bone. The elbows are held close to the body.

Body

The back is broad, firm, long, and level. The ribs are well sprung, and the chest is deep. The body is heavy and near to the ground.

Hindquarters

When viewed from behind, the rear is round and broad. The hindquarters are very powerful and well developed, with low hocks and well-bent stifles. The flank is well let down, showing no visible tuck-up.

Feet

Large, round, and covered with hair, the feet on the forelegs are slightly bigger than those on the hind legs.

Tail

Set on low, it should be carried level with the back. Well feathered.

Movement

Free and easy movement with good reach in front and powerful drive from behind. The Clumber's long body and short legs give him a characteristic rolling gait, which is a feature of the breed.

Coat

An abundant straight, silky coat lies close to the body with feathering on the chest and legs. The coat is weather resistant and is soft to the touch.

Color

A plain white body is preferred with slight lemon markings on the head and a freckled muzzle. Orange coloring is also permissible. The fewer the markings on the body the better, although a spot near the root of the tail is common.

Size

Males are 19–20 inches (48–50.5 cm) at the shoulder, females 17–19 inches (43–48 cm). The British standard gives an ideal weight for males of 80 pounds (36 kg) and females 65 pounds (29.5 kg). The American standard allows for a slightly heavier dog at the top limit—males should weigh between 70–85 pounds (31.75–38.5 kg), females between 55–70 pounds (25–31.75 kg).

LIVING WITH A CLUMBER SPANIEL

The Clumber Spaniel is perhaps the most low maintenance of the Spaniel breeds, with moderate exercise needs and a coat that is relatively easy to care for. He is an easygoing type and will make few demands. However, he may not be the best choice for the house proud.

The silky, white coat sheds profusely, particularly in the spring and the autumn. There is also the matter of drool—which can be quite evident in dogs with loose lip lines. The Clumber comes with one other warning—he does snore. . . .

Family Situation

This is one of the few Spaniel breeds that adapts to urban living. It is important that the Clumber's exercise requirements are not neglected, and he will appreciate the opportunity to use his nose. With a little effort, though, this can be provided in the city.

The Clumber Spaniel was often the choice of retired servicemen in the hunting field because of his tendency to stay close to his handler. In fact, the Clumber will be happy in all situations, from families with small children to senior citizens. This is a dog who loves people, and he will often bond closely with one person.

The great-hearted Clumber is well known for his sweet nature.

Training should be creative so the Clumber does not become bored.

The Clumber particularly likes dogs of his own kind, although he will live with all types. He is tolerant of small animals, although some owners have noted an antagonism toward cats.

The male is slightly bigger, and quite a bit heavier than the female, but, in temperament, there is little to choose between them.

Trainability

The Clumber Spaniel has a characteristic, thoughtful expression, and this is a fair reflection of his brain power. The Clumber Spaniel is a highly intelligent dog, and no task is too hard for him. He is quick to learn and seems to relish the challenge of a particularly difficult exercise. As you might expect, this goes hand in hand with the Clumber becoming easily bored. Training should be creative, with lots of variety and plenty of rewards.

The Clumber is a determined worker in the field, and this is reflected in all aspects of training. When a Clumber focuses on something, it can be very difficult to call him off until he thinks he has completed the job. He has

a tremendously powerful sense of smell, and he may become deaf to all calls when he is on a scent. However, the Clumber is very people oriented. If you build up a strong bond with your Clumber, he will turn to you for direction and will want to stay close by you.

Some say the Clumber has a stubborn streak, but, more often than not, this is a reaction to poor handling techniques. The Clumber Spaniel is a sensitive dog and does not need to be shouted at or pulled about in order to cooperate. If you resort to these methods, the Clumber will (quite rightly) dig in his heels.

Exercise

Do not be deceived by the Clumber Spaniel's heavy build—he does love his exercise, and although not fast in pace, he has the stamina to keep going all day. His favorite pastime is to use his powerful sense of smell to track interesting scents, and so he will appreciate a variety of walks over different terrain. Clumbers always want to carry something, and with a little training, you will get a good retrieve, which can form the basis of fun play sessions. Swimming is also excellent exercise. If you have access to a safe place where your Clumber can get in and out of the water easily, he will take great delight in retrieving from water.

Clumbers can be lazy, and they do enjoy their creature comforts. They do not need as much exercise as the other Spaniel breeds, which makes them a suitable choice for older people. It is important not to allow your Clumber to become too sedentary, or he will lose his *joie de vivre* as well as risk the serious health problems associated with obesity.

Grooming

A sparkling white Clumber Spaniel is an arresting sight, and the Clumber's straight, silky coat is easier to care for than the other Spaniel breeds. The feathering is moderate, restricted to the legs and chest, with light feather on the ears. You will need to allocate time to groom your Clumber Spaniel two or three times a week.

- Use a pin brush to groom the coat, working methodically from head to tail. You will find it easier if your Clumber lies on his side when you are working on his undercarriage.
- Repeat the process with a comb, paying particular attention to the feathering. If you come across a mat or a tangle, tease it out gently.
- If your Clumber is shedding his coat, you can use a metal rake, which is a good way of removing dead hair.
- You will need to trim hair that grows between the pads. You can also trim around the feet to neaten the appearance.
- Check the inside of the ears, and trim any excess hair, which will help to prevent ear infections.
- Obviously a white dog is going to get dirty, but do not be tempted to bathe your Clumber too often or you will destroy the natural oils in his coat. In most cases, mud will brush off easily once it has dried.
- Show dogs require a little more detailed preparation. The feather on the outer ear is trimmed using thinning scissors, and the hair behind the ear is also trimmed. The Clumber should look as natural as possible. Trimming around the feet, down from the hock joint, and on the underside of the tail is all that is required to tidy his appearance.

The Clumber is happy to take life at a leisurely pace, but his exercise needs should not be neglected.

Health Concerns

The Clumber Spaniel remains free from exaggeration and suffers few breed-specific conditions. However, breeders should guard against a tendency for dogs to become increasingly heavy, as this can lead to a lack of soundness.

Check out the following:

- **Hip dysplasia:** This remains a major concern in the breed with the Clumber Spaniel ranked fifth in OFA's breed listing showing incidence of the condition. From dogs tested from 1974 to the present day, 47.5 percent were found to be dysplastic (see page 22).
- **Entropion:** This has been prevalent in the breed, but there is evidence of some improvement in recent times (see page 23).
- **Ectropion:** This is rated as a minor problem in the Clumber Spaniel (see page 23).
- **Invertebral disk problems:** This has increased in incidence and is generally a result of producing heavier dogs.

The Clumber should be heavy in build but should not become overexaggerated.

- **Obesity:** It is all too easy for the laid-back Clumber to pile on the pounds—and this can lead to serious health problems. Owners are often fooled into thinking that the extra weight is OK for a natural heavyweight. It is best to take your Clumber to the vet and work out the best weight for his size. You can then monitor his weight with regular weigh-ins.

NEW CHALLENGES

The Clumber Spaniel enjoys using his brain. With training, this can be channeled in a number of different directions.

Hunting

The Clumber Spaniel is valued for his sense of smell and his habit of working close to the gun. He excels in dense undergrowth where there is plenty of game. He works at a steady pace (escaping injuries from brambles that faster dogs would suffer), and uses his nose to find hidden game. A powerful swimmer with big, webbed feet, the Clumber is an excellent water retriever. Newcomers to hunting often find the Clumber is a good choice as he works closely with his handler and is one of the easier breeds to train.

Obedience

A number of Clumber Spaniels have made their mark in obedience, but handlers do have their work cut out. The Clumber is very responsive to his handler, but he likes to think for himself, which can prove to be a challenge.

Agility

The Clumber is certainly not as agile or as fast as the other Spaniel breeds. He will learn to negotiate an agility course, and there are some Clumbers who have proved to be outstanding.

Tracking

This is a favorite of Clumbers, who love nothing better than following a scent. In the U.S., the first Clumber Spaniel earned the Variable Surface Tracker title in 1996, which shows what the breed is capable of.

Showing

A dedicated band of Clumber enthusiasts show their dogs at the very highest level. Presentation is relatively straightforward, but it is important to work at ring training. The Clumber must be motivated to perform so that he shows himself to best advantage.

Therapy Dogs

Clumber Spaniels are fairly low on registrations so not many work as therapy dogs. However, the breed's sweet, docile nature coupled with a calm outlook have proved ideal when visiting the sick and the elderly.

Cindy Brizes, from South Carolina, competes in agility with an unusual breed—a Clumber Spaniel called Merlin (Ch. Clussexx Crazy Like A Fox, CDX OA, AXJ).

"I had black-and-tan Coonhounds for many years, while my husband, Bill, had always been a German Shepherd person. However, when we were looking for a second dog, we decided to opt for a different breed. At the time, my husband was working with a woman in Washington State who owned a Clumber and he became intrigued by the breed. We started to find out as much as we could about Clumbers, and the more we discovered, the more the breed appealed to us.

"Merlin made an impact on the family from the minute we got him. His breeder, Doug Johnson, had warned us that Clumbers can be 'crazy' and he wasn't wrong! With the destruction of bushes, chewing of sprinkler heads, and the dragging of UPS packages through the doggy door, it quickly became apparent that Merlin would need something to challenge him and to distract him from other, more inappropriate behavior. I heard about agility at the obedience class I belonged to, and it seemed to be the perfect—if unusual—solution.

"I enrolled Merlin in a basic agility class, hoping to channel his energy, and he took to it immediately. Merlin is a dog who gives either 0 percent or 100 percent—nothing in-between. Agility was a great outlet for his 100 percent moments, and it really helped to boost his confidence. The running and jumping came fairly naturally to him, but he also thoroughly enjoyed conquering the more difficult obstacles, such as the teeter.

Continued on page 58

Merlin proves that Clumbers can do agility! The breed may not be the fastest, but he works closely with his handler and listens to instructions.

Continued from page 57

"Although Clumbers are rare in top-level agility—Merlin is the first to win an Excellent Agility title—there is no reason why they cannot take part in the sport; there's far more to it than winning. I think Merlin is proof that any breed can do well at agility, provided that they enjoy it. Merlin's success may be due to the fact that he is finer boned for a Clumber and I also keep a close eye on his weight, but more and more Clumbers are now becoming involved in the sport and doing very well.

"I don't think Clumbers can compete at the top level, for MACH titles, as they will probably lose out to the faster Border Collies and Shelties, but that's no reason to stop having fun! You just have to know your dog and breed and work within those constraints. For example, Merlin will give 100 percent when he's interested, but he tires quickly, so we have to keep practice sessions quite short—about 30 minutes or less.

Emerging from the tunnel and looking for the next obstacle. A reliable clear round in an agility run is always worth aiming for.

"We've also had to learn some dog psychology to overcome a few problems. When Merlin and I started competing at open level, he became painfully slow around the course. He was as fast as ever during training but not during trials. I used his jealousy of our Coonhound to solve the problem. Shortly before Merlin is due in the ring for a trial, Bill brings Merlin out to watch me walking the Coonhound and feeding him treats. Just at the last minute, Bill and I switch dogs and I take Merlin in the ring. Thanks to the jealousy factor, Merlin then runs like crazy and focuses intently on me.

"One of my best agility moments with Merlin was the day he won his first leg in Excellent Jumpers With Weaves. I was actually trying to finish his Open Standard title, but I entered him in excellent jumpers for the sheer heck of it; I never actually thought he would qualify because of the time constraint. It was his first time at this level, and he performed beautifully. We worked together as a team better than ever before and Merlin achieved a clear run under the course time. I couldn't believe it! I think it was then that I really started to believe that Merlin could achieve an Excellent title. He now has his AXJ title, and we are working on completion of his Excellent Standard title.

"Agility is incredible fun, not only for the dog but also for the handler. When Merlin and I are there in the ring and we are clicking as a team, I get so excited, I forget about everything else. I am so proud of Merlin, I could just cry. Of all the sports we have tried together (conformation, obedience, tracking, and agility), agility has built the biggest bond between us."

CHAPTER SIX

THE ENGLISH COCKER SPANIEL

The merry English Cocker Spaniel, with an ever-wagging tail, is the picture of fun and good humor. Busy and inquisitive, the English Cocker is always on the go, showing great enthusiasm and zest for life. At home, the English Cocker is loving, gentle, and affectionate, thriving on human company. He hates to be separated from his family and will pine if he is left alone for any length of time.

Bred to flush out game and to retrieve from land and from water, the English Cocker of today retains a strong hunting instinct and enjoys the opportunity to use his nose. He covers the ground effortlessly and has the stamina, if not the speed, of larger Spaniel breeds. Working English Cockers are still highly prized by sportsmen, although they tend to use exclusively field-bred lines.

The English Cocker is a compact, well-balanced dog. He is short in the leg, which allows for concentration of power as he moves. The head is beautifully sculptured, framed by long, feathered ears. The eyes are heart-stopping, with a melting expression of gentleness, but you can also see a sparkle that typifies the English Cocker's alert and active mind. English Cockers come in a full range of solid colors, parti-colors, and roans, with blue roans being the most popular, followed by blacks and reds.

If you want a fun-loving companion who enjoys life to the full, you can do no better than to choose an English Cocker Spaniel. He truly is a dog to suit all ages and types of owner.

BREED HISTORY

In the first part of the 19th century, Sporting Spaniels were named solely by the work they were suitable for. The Cocker or Cocking Spaniel was the name given to smaller dogs who were adept at flushing woodcock, and Land/Field Spaniels were the bigger dogs who were expert at springing game. There was little uniformity of size or type, and it was perfectly acceptable for breeders to offer Cockers and Field Spaniels from the same litter.

The situation was formalized with the advent of dogs shows in the mid-19th century when it was stipulated that Field Spaniels should weigh over 25 pounds (11 kg), and Cocker Spaniels under 25 pounds. To begin with, both types shared the same bloodlines, but over a period of time, breeders concentrated on producing specific types.

The most influential dog in the development of the Cocker Spaniel was Ch. Obo, who was born in June 1879. His sire was a Sussex Spaniel, and his dam was a Field Spaniel. Black in color, he had a long back and short legs and weighed 22 pounds (10 kg). He proved to be unbeatable in the show ring and went on to become a highly influential sire. Although he was referred to as a Field Spaniel, his influence on the Cocker breed was far reaching. His name appears on the pedigrees of more than half of the Cockers produced in the U.K. and the U.S. for the next 20 years. At that time, black was the dominant color in the show ring, but Ch. Obo was mated to bitches of all the Spaniel colors. He produced top-quality dogs in both solid colors and parti-colors.

One of Ch. Obo's most significant matings was to a bitch called Chloe II. She was mated to Obo in the U.K., and was then exported to the U.S. to give birth to her puppies. Among the resulting offspring was a male who was called Ch. Obo II. It was this dog that was the true founder of the breed in the U.S.

Gaining Recognition

In the U.K., the Cocker Spaniel was classified as a breed in its own right in 1892, and in 1902, the Cocker Spaniel Club was formed. Members quickly drew up an official breed standard, which remained unchanged for more than 50 years. Among the founding members was Mr. Farrow, the owner of Ch. Obo. Other important breeders at the time were Mr. Phillips, who owned the Rivington Kennel, working closely with Ch. Obo bloodlines, and Richard Lloyd, who founded the important "Of Ware" Kennel. The Cocker Spaniel quickly became established as a firm favorite in Britain, and soon its popularity spread worldwide.

Split in the Breed

In the United States, the influence of Ch. Obo II was still strong in the 1920s through his progeny, in particular a red dog called Robinhurst Foreglow. He was said to be the ideal Cocker, with longer legs and a more compact body than his illustrious ancestor.

Better known as a companion, the working English Cocker is still valued in the field.

The English Cocker should look sturdy and sporting, even if it is not a working dog.

However, there was a contingent in the U.S. that wanted to change the Cocker Spaniel, and this caused a major split in the breed, with the two factions specializing in their own "type" of Cocker. The English Cocker Spaniel Club of America was formed in 1936 to protect the interests of the original Cocker. After 10 years of fierce campaigning, they achieved their goal and the American Kennel Club (AKC) recognized two separate breeds—the American Cocker Spaniel (known in the U.S. as the Cocker Spaniel) and the English Cocker Spaniel.

THE ENGLISH COCKER SPANIEL TODAY

The English Cocker Spaniel is one of the most popular breeds in the U.K., ranked in third place with nearly 15,000 registrations a year. In the United States, the American Cocker is the popular choice, listed 15th by the AKC, with the English Cocker a distant 75th.

The English Cocker was originally valued as a shooting companion, but this has largely been usurped by his role as an outstanding companion dog. There are English Cockers who still work in the field, but these dogs tend to come from specifically field-bred lines. Working English Cockers are generally smaller than those bred for the show ring. They have much shorter coats, and their heads are plainer. It is customary to dock the tails of English Cockers, but those from the working strain usually have longer tails.

In the show ring, the English Cocker is one of the most glamorous of the Spaniel breeds, with only the American Cocker surpassing him for coat and elegance. Presentation is now of supreme importance (see page 66), and the show dog's coat would scarcely survive a day in the field. However, breeders must still adhere to the breed standard, which gives a picture in words of what the ideal English Cocker Spaniel should look like. Here is an outline of the British and American standards.

General Appearance

A sturdy, sporting dog who is compact and well balanced. He measures approximately the same from the withers to the ground, as from the withers to the root of the tail, according to the British standard, or the height from withers to the ground is slightly greater, according to the American standard.

Characteristics

Merry, with an ever-wagging tail, the English Cocker is alive with energy and has a typical bustling movement when he is following a scent.

Temperament

Affectionate and gentle, the English Cocker is full of life and is a faithful and engaging companion.

Head

Strong, yet free from coarseness, the head should be softly contoured. The muzzle is square, with a distinct stop midway between the nose and occiput. A well-developed skull is cleanly chiseled. The nose is wide for acute scenting power and is black, except in livers and liver parti-colors where it is brown.

Eyes

The English Cocker's expression is a feature of the breed. The eyes express gentleness and intelligence, but they are also wide awake, bright and merry. The eyes themselves are full but not prominent, with tight rims. The color is dark brown, but in the cases of liver, liver roan, and liver and white, it is dark hazel.

Ears

Another distinctive feature of the breed, the ears are set low, level with the eye. The leather is fine and should extend to the nose tip. The ears are covered with long, straight, silky hair.

Mouth

Strong jaws are capable of carrying game. The teeth should meet in a scissor bite (the upper teeth closely overlapping the lower teeth) according to the British standard or in a level bite (where the front teeth of the upper and lower jaws meet exactly edge to edge) according to the American standard.

Neck

Moderate in length, graceful, and muscular, set neatly into fine, sloping shoulders. A clean throat is required.

Forequarters

The shoulders are sloping and smooth fitting. The legs are strong, straight, and well boned. They should be sufficiently short to allow for concentrated power.

Body

Compact, giving an impression of strength without heaviness. The chest is deep, and the ribs are well sprung. The loin is short and wide, and the topline is firm and level, sloping gently from the end of the loin to the tail.

Hindquarters

Broad, well rounded, and muscular, the legs are well boned, there is a good bend of stifle, and the distance from the hock to the pad is short to allow for driving power.

The expression of gentleness is typical of the breed.

Feet

Firm, round, catlike feet, which are thickly padded.

Tail

The English Cocker's tail is set on lower than the line of the back, and it should be carried level. The merry action of the tail is a feature of the breed, and it should be active when the dog is moving.

Gait

Effortless ground-covering movement, showing great drive. There should be extension both in front and at the rear. The English Cocker carries his head proudly and maintains the same topline when he is moving as when he is standing.

Coat

The coat should be flat and silky—not too profuse and never curly. It is well feathered on the forelegs, body, and hind legs above the hocks.

The English Cocker bonds closely with all members of his family.

Color

Various. In solid colors, no white is allowed except on the chest.

Size

The American breed standard asks for a slightly bigger, heavier dog than the British version.
- **British standard:** Males 15.5–16 inches (39–40.5 cm), females 15–15.5 inches (38–39 cm). Weight 28–32 pounds (12.7–14.5 kg).
- **American standard:** Males 16–17 inches (40.5–43 cm), females 15–16 inches (38–43 cm). Weight—males 28–34 pounds (12.7–15.4 kg), females 26–32 pounds (11.8–14.5 kg).

LIVING WITH AN ENGLISH COCKER SPANIEL

The English Cocker Spaniel has a large fan base, and his compact size and cheerful disposition make him an ideal companion dog. Although his exercise needs are moderate, he has a labor-intensive coat, and owners will need to allocate the time for regular grooming sessions.

Family Situation

The Spaniel breeds are well known for their affinity with people, and this is particularly true of the English Cocker Spaniel. This is a loyal and loving breed who was put on Earth to be with people.

Ideally, the English Cocker should be in a home where he has to be left on his own for only limited periods. He is a true companion dog, wanting nothing more than to be part of the family, joining in with activities, or simply being in the same room and snuggling up for a stroke or a cuddle.

Interactions with young children should always be supervised, but the English Cocker is both gentle and playful and will happily find his place among the younger members of the family. The English Cocker Spaniel will also be a faithful friend to more elderly owners.

City or country living are equally acceptable to the adaptable English Cocker as long as he is given a varied and interesting routine. He gets on well with other dogs and has a special liking for other English Cockers. Most owners report that English Cockers are intensely curious of small animals, such as rabbits or guinea pigs, but they can be trained to ignore them.

If you want a good watchdog, the English Cocker will fit the bill. He will give an early-warning bark if people are approaching, but that is as far as his guarding duties go. All visitors will be greeted with boundless enthusiasm!

Trainability

Because the English Cocker Spaniel is generally easygoing and adaptable, there is a tendency to neglect his brains. This is an intelligent dog who will thrive on the stimulation of being given things to do. Training is not—and should not—be a boring repetition of basic exercises. This type of training is no better than a chore for you and your dog. The English Cocker is easily bored, and he will soon lose interest in you and will fail to cooperate.

Some owners report that their English Cocker has a stubborn streak, but this is more likely to be a response to uninspired training. Work at motivating your dog with tasty food treats—English Cockers love their food—and mix up training exercises with play sessions using a favorite toy. Most English Cockers love toys and are ready to present a "gift" at any given opportunity. Capitalize on this by playing retrieve games, which provide excellent mental and physical exercise. One word of warning, some English Cockers can become possessive over toys. If you see this trait in your dog, make sure you keep control of his toys and produce them specifically for play and training sessions.

Exercise

Field-bred English Cocker Spaniels tend to be lighter in build and generally have more stamina than their sturdier show counterparts. This does not mean that show-bred English Cockers are couch potatoes. This is a lively, active breed that is full of energy. The merry English Cocker is interested in everything that is going on, and his joy in life is characterized by his wagging tail when he is hot on the trail of an interesting scent.

An intelligent dog, the English Cocker needs mental stimulation.

The English Cocker is full of energy and thrives on the stimulation of being taken out for interesting expeditions.

It is important to provide interesting and stimulating exercise for your English Cocker Spaniel. You do not have to trudge for miles, but you must make sure that the outings are worth going on. If you have to miss out on a walk, make up for it with a play session in the backyard, which will tire your dog mentally and physically.

English Cockers are enthusiastic swimmers and will relish the opportunity for this type of exercise if you have access to a safe place.

Grooming

The adult English Cocker carries a reasonable amount of feathering, which will need to be groomed regularly. It is a good idea to accustom your pup to being groomed, even though he may not have a lot of coat, so that he learns to accept the attention without undue fuss.

- Use a soft brush for the head and body (this is also ideal to use on a puppy's coat).
- Follow this by going through the coat with a fine-toothed comb. This helps to remove dead hair, but if your dog is shedding, you may find a wide-toothed comb more effective.
- The feathering should be brushed with a metal pin brush and then combed with a wide-toothed comb, teasing out any mats or tangles.
- Use a pair of scissors to trim the excess hair that grows inside the ear. This aids air circulation and prevents ear infections.
- Trim the hair that grows between the pads.
- If you want to give the coat a glossy shine, finish by using a hand glove or a piece of velvet.

The American breed standard states: "Trimming is permitted to remove overabundant hair and to enhance the dog's true lines. It should be done so as to appear as natural as possible."

There is an art to preparing an English Cocker Spaniel for the show ring, and it takes a great deal of practice to get it right! Generally, exhibitors adhere to the following routine:

- The finger and thumb method of stripping out dead hair is used on the head, along the neck and shoulders, on the back, and on the sides of the body.
- Thinning scissors are used on the ears to reduce the bulk of the feathering and to ensure that the ears lie close to the head.
- The hair on the throat and on the chest will need to be trimmed.
- The upper thighs and the feathering on the hocks should be neatened up with scissors.
- The undercarriage is scissored to present a smooth outline.

The finger and thumb method is used to "pull" the coat.

Scissors are used trim excess hair so that the coat has a smooth outline.

- The tail will need a trim to tidy it up, and the feet will also need to be trimmed to give a round, catlike appearance.

Health Concerns

The English Cocker Spaniel is generally sound in mind and body, although there has been some concern in recent times over temperament (see "Canine Rage Syndrome").

- **Progressive retinal atrophy:** This has been a cause of major concern in the breed, and all breeding stock should be eye tested (see page 23).
- **Cataracts:** These can occur, but the number of affected dogs is low (see page 23).
- **Familial nephritis:** A fatal condition caused by shrunken kidneys. Cases were reported in the breed, but fortunately, due to the efforts of breeders to eliminate the problem, it is now rare.
- **Canine rage syndrome:** This is a condition where a normally placid dog inexplicably attacks and later seems unaware of his behavior. The condition, which may be inherited, has a higher incidence in red and gold English Cockers. However, suspect bloodlines have been avoided, and cases are increasingly rare. To date, the most effective treatments are diet change, vitamin supplementation, and hormone therapy.
- **Hip dysplasia:** According to the OFA's findings, the English Cocker is ranked 111th in listings showing the incidence of the condition, with 5.7 percent of dogs tested proving to be affected. It is therefore of only minor significance, but breeding stock should be tested.
- **Congenital deafness:** A survey carried out in the United States has shown that approximately 3 percent of English Cockers may suffer congenital deafness in one or both ears.
- **Obesity:** Resist those pleading eyes that say, "I haven't eaten for months," and remember that obesity can lead to serious health problems.

The English Cocker is a fast and enthusiastic competitor in agility.

NEW CHALLENGES

A talented and versatile dog, the English Cocker Spaniel is ready to try anything—and can achieve considerable success in many areas.

Hunting

Originally bred to flush woodcock—a shy bird that hides in the undergrowth—the English Cocker is now more of an all-around hunter, flushing and retrieving game and rabbit. He is bred to cover the ground, working through the densest cover and using his acute sense of smell.

The English Cocker is not a hard-flushing dog but is a busy, methodical worker who will flush game at the very last second. The English Cocker has a very soft mouth and is a careful and reliable retriever.

Obedience

This is a discipline where English Cockers can be successful as they do not work at too fast a pace and can achieve the accuracy that is required. However, motivation can be a problem, and training needs to be varied and stimulating.

Agility

There are a number of English Cockers who have taken to agility. Although they cannot compete with the faster dogs, they turn in good clear rounds on a regular basis.

Tracking

The English Cocker Spaniel has an excellent sense of smell, and competing in this discipline is an extension of his natural ability at hunting.

Showing

The merry English Cocker is a popular show dog, and the goal to aim for is to have a neatly presented dog—looking as natural as possible—and moving across the ring with an effortless gait and with an ever-wagging tail.

Therapy Dogs

Gentle and loving, the English Cocker Spaniel is ideally suited to therapy work. It is important that breeders continue to work hard at maintaining the excellent temperament, which is so much a hallmark of the breed.

Bea Chugkowski, from Massachusetts, is a dedicated worker for Cocker Spaniel Rescue of New England (CSRNE). In her role, she has encountered many special (albeit troubled) dogs, but none more so than her adopted English Cocker Spaniel, Marco Polo. Here, Bea describes how flyball became the catalyst for Marco Polo's change from an abused, frightened dog to a confident, beloved pet.

"I got my first dog, Jake, a Cocker Spaniel (American), from CSRNE and have stayed in touch with the organization ever since, gradually becoming a bit more involved in the work that they do.

"Jake was quite demanding at first, so I enrolled him in obedience classes and changed him from a superdominant dog to a supercompetitive dog who was also a wonderful pet. It was at obedience classes that I first found out about flyball. I thought it was an ideal way to exercise Jake during the winter, and it wasn't long before both of us fell in love with the speed of the sport. I continued with flyball even after Jake retired.

"When Marco Polo arrived at CSRNE, he was severely underweight, had been beaten and strangled, and possessed absolutely no socialization skills. There was very little about the world that he understood. He wasn't housetrained, he was terrified of nearly everything—grass, people in bulky clothes, men . . . anything that wasn't familiar.

"So the lengthy process of socialization and training began. Marco was put on a strict schedule, with the hope that consistency would lead to familiarity, and familiarity would result in confidence. It was not a quick process, but, after a few months, he was ready to 'go public' and receive further training at a local obedience training class.

"Initially, he found it completely overwhelming—even a stranger looking at him could reduce him to a quivering wreck. However, slowly but surely, and with the help of an awful lot of cookies, he began to come out of his shell. After a year, he amazed us all by passing his Canine Good Citizen test.

"Marco still had a long way to go, however. He was still skittish and terribly undersocialized. I wanted to broaden his experiences, and as I had another dog starting flyball, I decided to enroll Marco as well. I never

Continued on page 70

© Jo-Ann Gerde

Marco Polo flies the hurdle, tennis ball in mouth, as he returns to his handler. English Cockers thrive on the excitement of a flyball contest.

FLYING WITH MARCO POLO

Continued from page 69
expected him to become a 'real' flyball dog—he wouldn't retrieve, couldn't catch, was terrified of the box, and refused to leave my side. My other dog was ready to race in six months. Marco certainly wasn't. However, he did seem to like running over the jumps, so we persisted. After a year, he could run over the four jumps and back.

"Involving the tennis ball was a lot harder. Marco took some convincing that the 'evil' flyball box would not attack him. Teaching him to retrieve the ball from the box took another year and involved many a night tossing popcorn in the air to encourage his catching skills as well as soaking tennis balls in chicken broth to make them more appealing.

"By the time Marco had mastered the different elements of flyball, we were more than three years into training. Hearts in throats, we decided to enter him into a tournament. The first was not a success. Marco hated the unfamiliar, highly polished floor and refused to run. The second tournament, however, was a triumph!

With patience and understanding, Marco Polo has now become a confident and much-loved member of Bea's family.

"I had no ambitions for Marco that day. I didn't expect him to win. All I hoped for was a clean run. That would be enough and would make me so proud. He ran 20 heats that day. The first 19 were unsuccessful. Finally, however, during the very last heat, Marco successfully completed a clean run. I was ecstatic, and the whole room cheered. Marco had his first flyball point. It was the start of something special.

"At the next tournament, it was as if Marco suddenly understood the whole concept of flyball, and he left that day having earned the title of Flyball Dog (FD). The team threw a party to celebrate. At the tournament following that, Marco stunned everyone by running every heat cleanly with no mistakes. Recently, he ran flawlessly at a completely unfamiliar venue and set a new personal-best time of 6.9 seconds as well as achieving his FDX title (Flyball Dog Excellent).

"I am exceptionally proud of Marco for his achievements but, far more important than the titles he has earned, is the fact that my scared little dog has become a fairly confident and rather charming pet."

CHAPTER SEVEN

THE ENGLISH SPRINGER SPANIEL

© Janet Martin

A sporting dog of character and purpose, the English Springer Spaniel has won the hearts and minds of canine enthusiasts all over the world. The combination of balance, poise, and symmetry; the melting expression of his dark eyes; and his sweet, docile nature make him a favorite with all types of owners.

If you are looking for a working dog, the English Springer has much to offer. He has boundless energy and enthusiasm, and will hunt, flush, and retrieve on land and from water. He is equipped to work in rough conditions—in brambles and thorns—and can cover the ground at breakneck speed.

As a companion, the English Springer is the ideal choice for a lively family who enjoy an action-packed lifestyle. A natural enthusiast, the English Springer loves to be involved in everything that is going on and will repay his owners with his very special devotion and loyalty. He gets on well with children of all ages and will not pick a fight with other dogs.

An alert and intelligent dog, the English Springer tunes into his owner and is eager to please. He thrives on all training challenges that come his way.

The English Springer is the longest in the leg of the land Spaniels and has an active, racy build. He is a perfectly balanced dog and conveys an impression of strength and endurance. The head, with the long, feathered ears and large, kind eyes, is stunning. This is a breed that looks equally spectacular on the sporting field or in the show ring.

Among English Springer Spaniel fans, liver and white is probably the most popular color, although black and white English Springers also have a big following. Both these colors may have tan markings. The coat is moderately feathered and can be maintained with regular grooming.

For a breed that combines good looks, sporting ability, energy, enthusiasm, gentleness, and devotion, the English Springer is, quite simply, the best.

BREED HISTORY

The term "Springer" is the perfect description for Sporting Spaniels who specialized in springing or flushing out game. On large country estates in England, larger Springer Spaniels were used to flush out game for the gun, the net, the hawk, or the hound. These docile dogs, with ever-wagging tails, were valued for working in harmony with birds and other dogs.

A number of landowners developed their own strain of Sporting Spaniel, and the Norfolk Spaniel is clearly an ancestor of the modern English Springer. These liver and white dogs, bred by the Duke of Norfolk in the 1800s, were expert at hunting as well as springing game. Even better, they would retrieve fallen game from land or from water. It was this versatility that was the making of the English Springer and is why the breed is the first choice of so many sportsmen today.

The old English Water Spaniel, which is now extinct as a breed, is also thought to have played a part in the development of the English Springer. Sir Hugo Fitzherbert bred both Norfolk Spaniels and English Water Spaniels and produced many champions. English Water Spaniels were slightly larger than the Springer Spaniels then in vogue, and it is said that one of his champions was a straight cross between a Cocker Spaniel and an English Setter.

The first pure strain of English Springer Spaniels can be traced back to the 1800s. The Boughey family, based in Aqualate, Shropshire, U.K., started their own breeding program with a stud book recording the litters they bred, dating back to 1813. The family kept the strain going for over a century. In 1903, they bred

As the name implies, the English Springer is expert at flushing or springing game and then retrieving it to hand.

© Rich Russeff

Field Trial Champion Velox Poder, whose pedigree can be traced through the Aqualate stud book, going back to Mop I, who was whelped in 1812.

Official Recognition

The official history of the English Springer Spaniel starts in 1902 when the Spaniel breeds were officially separated and classified. The English Springer was separated from the smaller Cocker Spaniels and also from its Welsh counterpart—the Welsh Springer Spaniel. In 1903, the first class specifically for English Springers was scheduled at a dog show. In 1906, Beechgrove Will, a liver and white dog, became the first champion in the breed.

In the United States, English Springers were used as hunting dogs throughout the 19th century. They worked in swamplands and in rough brambly terrain, flushing and retrieving wildfowl. Popularity of the breed dipped for a time when Setters and Pointers proved highly

© Janet Martin

There are notable differences between the English Springers bred in the United States (left) and the breed in its native land (below).

successful at hunting quail. As the pheasant developed as a game bird, the English Springer came into his own again.

Following official recognition in England, the first English Springer Spaniel was registered with the American Kennel Club in 1910. The English Springer Spaniel Field Trial Association was formed in 1924, and this became the parent club for the breed in the United States.

THE ENGLISH SPRINGER SPANIEL TODAY

The English Springer Spaniel is becoming increasingly popular on both sides of the Atlantic. It is ranked 27th in AKC listings, with annual registrations of 9,128. In the U.K., it is the fourth most popular breed, with 13,877 registrations a year.

Devotees of the breed are determined that the English Springer remains true to type—a typical working dog as well as a glamorous show dog. However, in recent times, there has been a marked divergence in type in English Springers bred in America as working dogs and those bred for the show ring. The working fraternity favors a lighter dog with shorter ears and less feathering. Color is of less importance, with irregular patches and ticking being perfectly acceptable. As well as being bigger and heavier, the American show dog is shorter in the body with a sloping topline. The tail set is higher, and the tail is sometimes carried above the level of the back—which is considered a major fault among British breeders. In terms of color, a dark saddle over the back against a pure white background is favored.

Feelings reached a pitch in 1993 when the English Springer Spaniel Club voted for separation from the American breed club, claiming that American-bred dogs should be considered as a separate breed. To date, no action has been taken, but the debate remains a burning issue in the breed.

In fact, the American breed standard differs very little from the British version, although it gives a much fuller description. Here is an outline of what the ideal English Springer should look like according to the two breed standards.

General Appearance

A compact, symmetrically built dog of medium size, he is strong and muscular, active and racy, and is every inch a Sporting Spaniel.

Breed Characteristics

A merry dog who conveys an impression of power, endurance, and agility. Style, symmetry, balance, and enthusiasm are his hallmarks.

Temperament

The English Springer has a happy disposition and is friendly with everyone he meets. He is docile and eager to please.

Head

He has a medium-length skull, fairly broad and slightly rounded. As the skull rises from the foreface, it makes a stop divided by a groove between the eyes. The muzzle is approximately the same length as the skull and half the width. The cheeks are flat, and the nostrils are well developed. The nose is liver or black, depending on the dog's color.

Eyes

Medium-sized, almond-shaped eyes are set fairly wide apart and deep in their sockets. The expression is kindly and alert.

Ears

Long, fairly wide, and hanging close to the cheeks, ears should not be so long as to be a

The typical expression of the English Springer is kindly and alert.

hindrance to a working dog. The correct ear set is level with the eye. Ears should be nicely feathered.

Mouth

The jaws are strong, and the teeth should meet in a perfect scissor bite (upper teeth closely overlapping lower teeth).

Neck

A good length of neck should be strong and muscular with no hint of throatiness. The neck should be slightly arched, tapering toward the head and blending gradually and smoothly into sloping shoulders.

Forequarters

The forelegs should be straight and well boned. The shoulders are sloping and well laid, sloping smoothly into the contour of the body. The elbows are set close to the body, and the pasterns are short, strong, and flexible.

The build of an English Springer is compact and symmetrical.

Body

The body is strong and firm, and the length (from shoulder to buttock) is slightly greater than the height at the withers. The chest is deep, reaching to the level of the elbows. The ribs are well sprung, and the loin is muscular and slightly arched.

Hindquarters

The rear assembly should appear firm and muscular, conveying an impression of strength and driving power. The thighs are broad and well developed; the stifles and hocks are moderately bent.

Feet

The feet are tight and compact. They should be round in shape with strong pads.

Tail

The tail is low set, and according to the British standard, it is never carried above the level of the back. The American standard asks for the tail to be carried horizontally or slightly elevated. Both standards agree that the tail has a characteristic merry, lively action and is well feathered.

Movement

The Springer's movement is a test of his soundness and conformation and is unique to the breed. The forelegs swing straight forward from the shoulder, throwing the feet forward in an easy, free manner. The hocks drive from behind, coming well under the body, following the line of the forelegs. In profile, the Springer shows a long, ground-covering stride and carries a firm back.

Coat

Weather-resistant coat consisting of a short, dense undercoat and a straight top coat lying close to the body. There should be moderate feathering on the ears, forelegs, body, and hindquarters.

Color

Liver and white, black and white, or either of these colors with tan markings. Blue or liver roan.

Size

Height at the withers is approximately 20 inches (51 cm) for males, 19 inches (48 cm for females). Weight: 50 pounds (22.5 kg) for males, 40 pounds (18 kg) for females.

LIVING WITH AN ENGLISH SPRINGER

An English Springer Spaniel will be a lively addition to any family. He fits in with most lifestyles, but new owners should be aware of his special needs.

Family Situation

The English Springer Spaniel is an adaptable dog and will thrive in the city or in the country—provided you can give him the exercise and stimulation that he needs. This a dog with a natural *joie de vivre*, and he needs the space to run and to express his exuberant nature.

The English Springer Spaniel loves people, and he is always ready to join in with children's games. He may be a little too boisterous for very small children, but with careful supervision, he will be an affectionate and sensitive companion.

Bred to work alongside other dogs, the English Springer is a sociable type who enjoys canine company. He is tolerant of small animals, and some owners note a special affinity for cats.

The male Springer is slightly bigger and quite a bit heavier than the female. In terms of temperament, the male is probably the most devoted, with females showing a slightly more independent streak.

Trainability

The English Springer is a joy to train, as he instinctively wants to please. Quick to learn, he will pick up instructions in no time, and he thrives on being given new tasks to learn. However, this is a breed that can become easily bored, and so it is important to guard against monotonous repetition. A naturally curious dog, the English Springer has an active mind that can jump around a bit, so it is important to keep your dog focused and motivated with lots of praise and reward. Never use harsh methods to correct your Springer. He will be easily cowed and will become too worried and anxious to work for you.

Some English Springers can be headstrong, and there are those who have quite an independent side to their characters. Very often, it is a case of enthusiasm running away with them. The excitement of finding a new scent, for example, can drive out all other considerations. The best plan is to start training from an early stage so that your dog becomes focused on you and will ignore other distractions. The recall is the most important exercise to teach so that you can be confident to let your dog off lead, knowing he will always return to you. The trick is to make yourself as interesting as possible (by having treats or a toy at the ready) so your English Springer wants to come back to you.

A playful dog who is always on the lookout for a game.

© Janet Martin

Boundless energy and enthusiasm are hallmarks of the breed.

© D. Shields

Retrieving is a strong instinct in English Springers. Most love to play retrieve games and will delight in having something to carry. Playing retrieve is also a good way of interacting with your dog on a walk so he sees that you are a fun person to be with.

Exercise

Do not choose an English Springer unless you are prepared to give him the regular exercise that should be considered essential. This is a high-energy dog that likes nothing better than running, working his way through undergrowth, and investigating every scent he comes across. If there is a stretch of water, the English Springer will be keen to take a dip.

If you are an active, outdoors person, there is no better companion, but do not make the mistake of thinking that the English Springer will be content with limited exercise. He will quickly become bored and restless. Being a clever dog, he will soon invent mischief of his own to allay his boredom.

English Springer owners should plan to give two lengthy walks (30 minutes or more) or three shorter walks (minimum of 20 minutes) per day. For a special treat, take your Springer for a really long outing, walking over different types of terrain, so that your dog can run and follow scents to his heart's content.

Grooming

The English Springer has a medium-length, silky coat with moderate feathering. He grows an undercoat, but the extent of this will depend on his home environment. The amount of feathering may also vary from dog to dog.

Working and companion dogs require regular grooming—at least twice weekly—and some trimming. The show dog needs extensive preparation before he is exhibited in the ring.

• A bristle brush should be used on the coat, working methodically from head to tail.
• A fine-toothed comb is needed for the shorter hair on the body.
• A wider, open-toothed comb should be used on the feathering.
• A medium-toothed rake is useful for teasing out tangles, which tend to form behind the ears, in the armpits, and between the hindlegs.
• Depending on the amount of coat and feathering, the English Springer will generally need trimming every three months. The areas that need attention are the feathering on the ears (this can be trimmed one-third of the way down), inside the ears, around the feet, and between the toes and pads. The feathering on the tail can also be tidied up.

The Show Dog

The show dog requires considerable ongoing attention. In the United States, presentation is very important, and great skill is needed to groom a show dog.

• The finger and thumb method is used to pull out dead hair from the head and from the body (where a comb or rake can also be used, with the aim of presenting smooth contours).
• Thinning scissors are used to tidy the feathering on the ears. They should not be overtrimmed as this gives a harsh appearance.

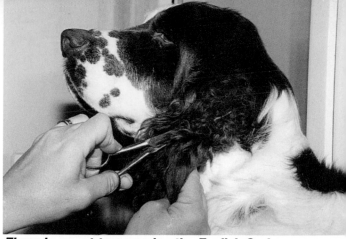

There is an art to preparing the English Springer for the show ring.

• The neck and throat are the only part of the body where clippers can be used to achieve a smooth outline.
• Straight-edged scissors are used on the legs, and the hair around the feet should be trimmed to give a round, compact shape.
• The feathering on the tail needs to be tidied, and the hair from the hock to the pastern joint is scissored to give a neat appearance.

Health Concerns

The English Springer Spaniel is a breed that is built without exaggeration, and he suffers few breed-specific problems. Eye conditions are probably the biggest area of concern. Be aware of the following:

• **Retinal dysplasia:** Check this out with the breeder. The disease is easy to control due to its method of inheritance and early diagnosis (see page 23).
• **Progressive retinal atrophy:** This is a concern among English Springer breeders as it is a condition that can be carried by clinically normal dogs (see page 23).
• **Entropion:** This is a minor issue in the breed, and affected dogs can be corrected with surgery (see page 23).

- **Hip dysplasia:** Ranked 61st in the OFA breed list, with a percentage of 14.3 in dogs tested from 1974 to the present day (see page 22).
- **Elbow dysplasia:** Ranked 14th in the OFA breed list. Of 526 evaluations, 86.3 percent were normal, 13.7 percent were dysplastic. Of these, 10.6 percent were Grade 1; 2.3 percent were Grade 2; and 0.8 percent were Grade 3 (see page 22).
- **Patellar luxation:** Ranked 18th in the OFA breed list. Of 51 dogs tested, 94.1 percent were normal and 5.9 percent were affected (see page 22).
- **Canine rage syndrome:** This condition, where the dog becomes aggressive

The English Springer is active and athletic and can work in areas that would be difficult for heavier breeds, such as Labrador Retrievers.

momentarily—and for no apparent reason, has been seen in some American-bred dogs. To date, diet change and hormone therapy have proved the most effective treatments.

NEW CHALLENGES

The English Springer Spaniel has always been highly prized for his versatility as a hunting dog, but this also translates into many of the canine disciplines.

Hunting

The English Springer Spaniel is a superb hunter, and his forte is pheasants. He is built to cover the ground effortlessly and with great speed, and this gives a hard-driving flush that springs pheasants for the gun. The English Springer will work over all types of terrain and is in his element when he is in the midst of a thicket, searching out hidden game. When asked, he is a reliable retriever of waterfowl. English Springers can be trained to a very high standard, and many compete successfully in field trials.

Sniffer Dogs

An excellent sense of smell and a persistence when tracking a scent have made the English Springer the preferred breed for drugs and arms detection work. His light, athletic build means that he can get to inaccessible places that bigger dogs find more difficult, and his endless desire to work has proved a great bonus.

Tracking

This competitive sport makes use of the English Springer's scenting ability, and he has proved to be a happy and willing worker.

Agility

The lightning-fast English Springer relishes the sport of agility. His enthusiasm can sometimes get the better of him, and handlers need to work hard at contact points marked on the obstacles or the English Springer will record a flying time but pick up penalties for faults.

Obedience

This is a sport where precision and accuracy are all important. Although the English Springer can be trained to a high level and has proved very successful, he may become bored by the relatively slow and sedate nature of the work.

Showing

The English Springer makes a spectacular sight in the show ring, and his effortless gait is his hallmark. Presentation is all-important, and handlers need to work hard at all aspects of ring training. The most important consideration is to make showing fun and to bring out the English Springer's natural air of showmanship.

There is no greater fun for the English Springer than flying round an agility course.   © Janet Martin

Therapy Dogs

One of the most delightful aspects of the English Springer Spaniel's temperament is his sweet and affectionate nature. Despite his natural exuberance, the English Springer has a special sensitivity toward people, which makes him a wonderful therapy dog.

BOMB BUSTER

Staff Sergeant Danny Morgan has spent 17 years in the British army. He is currently a member of the Royal Army Veterinary Corps, working as part of the 101 Military Working Dog Support Unit. For the last five years, he has worked alongside English Springer Spaniel Buster, an arms explosive search dog. Buster and Danny's heroic exploits in the war on terror have made headline news on several occasions.

"Buster is originally from a rescue center, which is how most army dogs are selected. He may have started off as an unwanted pet, but he is certainly wanted now! As a dog handler, you can often have several dogs under your control at one time, all at different levels of training, but Buster and I developed such a strong bond that he now lives at home as a family pet with me, my wife Nicki, and our daughter Emma.

Continued on page 82

Continued from page 81

"Military working dog training is very intensive. There's a lot more to it than the dog just finding something and alerting his handler. However, Buster showed a lot of potential during training, and he's certainly lived up to that early promise. He really enjoys his job because I think he sees it as a game. For Buster, it's a case of retrieving guns and ammunition instead of the usual balls and sticks."

Buster has proven so successful at his job that he was invited to take part in a search demonstration held by the armed forces at Portsmouth's naval base as part of the Queen's golden jubilee celebration in 2002. "Dogs are not normally allowed on naval bases, so a lot of strings had to be pulled to get special permission for Buster to take part in this event," said Danny.

However, Buster's most famous result came in 2003 when he detected a large cache of weaponry and ammunition in the village of Safwan, southern Iraq. The operation was part of a dawn raid on enemy properties. Danny recalls, "The soldiers had found nothing, so I unleashed Buster to see if he would detect anything. Within minutes, he became very excited and I knew he'd discovered something. The Iraqis had gone to great lengths to hide their weapons, but Buster still managed to find them. Without Buster, those weapons would have been a threat against the troops and local civilian population."

Buster was awarded the Dickin Medal (the animal equivalent of the Victoria Cross) for his services in Iraq. He was also given the Crufts Hero Dog Of The Year Award in 2005. Danny says, "It means the world to me. For a young lad that joined the army and a rescue dog to win the first hero award is fantastic. I'm very proud of him. He's my overall hero." This is a sentiment obviously shared by the entire family, as Danny explains. "Whenever Buster and I go away on an operation, Emma gets terribly upset. When I went to Iraq, she was devastated because she didn't know if he'd be coming back. When we're on duty, she sends him more treats than me!"

Buster and Danny remain in active service and continue to defend their country. Danny hopes that Buster will live out a long and happy life with him and his family. As he says in conclusion, "Buster's my best friend."

Buster, an English Springer Spaniel, with Staff Sergeant Danny Morgan, was once a candidate for rescue. Today Buster is a canine hero, serving with distinction as an arms explosive search dog.

CHAPTER EIGHT

THE FIELD SPANIEL

Noble, fun loving, sensitive, and unusually docile—these are the words that are most frequently used to describe the Field Spaniel. A true hunter, this is a breed that thrives on a long, hard day in the field rather than being a stay-at-home pet. In fact, the English breed standard specifically states, "Ideal for rough shooting or companion for the country dweller. Not suitable for city."

Although the Field Spaniel loves the outdoor life, he is still a most affectionate companion and bonds closely with his family. He is gentle with children and thrives on the companionship of people of all ages. He likes to be busy. If there is nothing much happening, a Field will find a toy and come toward you, tail wagging, asking for a game. However, this is a breed that also has an independent streak, and as a result, he is not quite as needy as some of the other Spaniel breeds.

In terms of appearance, the Field Spaniel is a medium-sized dog of substance who retains an athletic build. He is slightly longer than he is tall, with strong legs and characteristically large feet. His finest feature is his head, which is beautifully chiseled and framed by long, low-set ears. The eyes, which range in color from dark hazel to dark brown, are large and expressive, conveying a look of gravity and gentleness.

Field Spaniels can be black, liver, or roan (with or without tan points). The coat is long and silky with abundant feathering.

Of all the Spaniels, it is the Field Spaniel that combines beauty with utility, and it is this quality that makes the breed so special.

BREED HISTORY

Land or Field Spaniels were popular working dogs on country estates in Britain. The dogs were bred for their ability to perform in the field: finding and flushing out game and then retrieving it from the land or from water. There was little uniformity in terms of appearance. It was not until the sport of dog showing came to the fore in the mid-19th century that attempts were made to categorize the different types of Spaniels into specific breeds.

Those who favored Land Spaniels wanted to create their own special breed that would stand out in the show ring. Pioneers decided to aim for a large, all-black Spaniel that was capable of working in the field as well as retrieving from land and water. There were close links with the Cocker Spaniels, and in the early days, dogs from the same litter would be identified as different breeds. For example, small black dogs (under 25 pounds/11 kg) were referred to as Cocker Spaniels, and larger black dogs were known as Field Spaniels.

The Field Spaniel was recognized as a separate breed in the 1880s, and in 1894 Coleshill Rufus became the first Field Spaniel to be registered with the American Kennel Club. Interestingly, he was a liver-colored dog—so the plan to specialize in all-black dogs was short-lived. In those early days of the breed, a breeder called Dr. Spugin campaigned for the recognition of colored Field Spaniels. He had a liver roan and tan Spaniel called Alonzo who proved to be an influential stud dog. His name can be seen in many of the pedigrees of early Field Spaniels—and Cocker Spaniels.

Just as Field Spaniels were becoming successfully established, disaster struck. Sussex Spaniel bloodlines were used in an attempt to make the Field Spaniel heavier in bone and more low set. This was the type that judges seemed to favor in the show ring. In a remarkably short time, though, the breed was virtually destroyed. By the 1900s, the Field Spaniel had become so exaggerated that it had virtually lost all resemblance to the original concept of a Sporting Spaniel. The dogs that were produced were long in body, low to the

Coverwell Davey's Double showing the working ability that is a hallmark of the breed.

ground, and so heavy that they could never have carried out a day's work in the field. In a bid to breed for this new type, Basset Hound bloodlines were used, but the resulting dogs were so grotesquely exaggerated that they soon fell from favor. An American champion was recorded in 1916, and it was to be more than 50 years before another Field Spaniel achieved that honor.

Breed Revival

The story of the Field Spaniel followed similar lines in the U.K. With the added impact of two World Wars, numbers fell so dramatically that the breed was close to extinction.

Fortunately, there were a few dedicated British breeders who still had the dream of producing a strong Sporting Spaniel who could work in the thickest of cover. They realized that they needed a more upstanding, athletic type of dog, and they decided to introduce English Springer Spaniel bloodlines. It took time to achieve their purpose, and all resulting offspring that were used for breeding were selected for their working ability. In this way, the breed was

The Field Spaniel is a medium-sized, well-balanced, hunting dog. It is heavier in build than the Cocker and Springer breeds, but it should appear active and athletic.

restored to its original purpose, and a larger Spaniel that was longer in the leg, but with the substance and movement of the original Field Spaniels, emerged. The new type of Field Spaniel also retained the typical head that was a feature of the early dogs.

There were some drawbacks to the English Springer bloodlines, mostly in terms of color. It was obviously important to maintain the difference between Field Spaniels and English Springers, and so the breed standard was changed to disqualify liver and white or black-and-white Field Spaniels.

It was still a struggle to reestablish the breed. Numbers were so small that the English Kennel Club withdrew championship status in the 1950s. This was restored in 1969 only after determined efforts by British breeders to put the Field Spaniel back on the map.

Back in the U.S.

In December 1966, a litter of Field Spaniels, bred by Mrs A. M. Jones of the Mittina Kennels in the U.K., were born. Three of the puppies were imported to America, and these dogs went on to be the foundation of the breed in its new form. The three dogs were: Mac (Ch. Pilgrim of Mittina), Twiggy (Ch. Flowering May of Mittina), both owned by Richard and Doris Squier, and Brig (Ch. Brigadier of Mittina) owned by P. Carl Tuttle. If you research extended pedigrees of Field Spaniels in the United States today, you will almost certainly see the names of these original imports.

THE FIELD SPANIEL TODAY

Today, the Field Spaniel has a select but highly dedicated following. It is currently ranked 132nd in the AKC listings, with annual registrations of 133. In the U.K., the Field Spaniel comes in at number 143, with annual registrations of 75. The breed is highly valued for its beauty and for its working ability and is the preferred choice of many sportsmen.

The Field Spaniel has undergone some dramatic changes during its short history, but the breed standard describes the ideal dog who will achieve honors in the show ring and will also be capable of working in the field.

There may be slight variations in the wording of the breed standard, depending on the national governing canine body. However, this is a broad outline of a typical Field Spaniel.

General Appearance

A well-balanced, medium-sized hunter/companion, he is built for activity and endurance. He has a noble, upstanding bearing.

Breed Characteristics

This is a sporting dog who is ideal for rough shooting and working in heavy cover and water.

Temperament

Unusually docile and sensitive, he is also independent and fun loving.

Head

Conveys the impression of high breeding, character, and nobility. A well-developed skull has a pronounced, rounded occiput. The head is well chiseled with straight, clean cheeks. The brows are slightly raised. The stop is moderate, and the muzzle is long and lean, curving from the nose to the throat. The nose is large and fleshy with open nostrils and can be light to dark brown or black, depending on the coat color.

The head gives an impression of nobility and high breeding.

Eyes

Almond shaped and set moderately wide apart. The color is dark hazel to dark brown, and the expression is grave and gentle.

Ears

Moderately long (reaching the end of the muzzle), wide, set on low (just below eye level), and well feathered.

Mouth

Strong jaws have close-fitting lips, and teeth meet in a perfect scissor bite (upper teeth closely overlapping lower teeth).

Neck

Long, strong, and muscular so the dog can retrieve game without undue fatigue, slightly arched, and set well into the shoulders.

Forequarters

Long, sloping shoulders, are well laid back. Legs are straight and of moderate length.

Body

The neck slopes smoothly into the withers, and the back is level and muscular. The chest is deep and well developed (equal in depth to the front leg from elbow to ground), and the rib cage is two-thirds of the body length.

Hindquarters

Strong and driving, stifle and hocks are moderately bent and hocks are close to the ground.

Feet

Tight, round, webbed feet have strong pads. Large feet are a characteristic of the breed.

Tail

Set on low and never carried above the level of the back. Nicely feathered with a lively action, slanting down when at rest. The tail is customarily docked to one-third.

Movement

The head is held high and alert, and strong forward action is coupled with great drive from the rear, producing a long, unhurried stride.

Coat

A single coat is moderately long, dense, and weather resistant. It is silky and glossy and can be flat or wavy, with Setter-like feathering on the chest, underbody, and back of the legs but clean from the hocks to the ground.

Color

Black, liver, golden liver, roan, or any of these colors with tan points is fine. A small amount of white on the chest is allowed.

Size

Males 18 inches (45.5 cm) at the shoulder, females 17 inches (43 cms). Weight 40–55 pounds (18–25 kg).

The Field Spaniel loves his family—if there are children around, that is an added bonus.

LIVING WITH A FIELD SPANIEL

The Field Spaniel is an easy breed to care for. However, you must be aware of his particular needs so that you can be confident that you can provide the home he will be happy in.

Family Situation

Bred for country living, the Field Spaniel is a hardy, rugged type who does not really adapt to an urban environment. Given that stipulation, the Field is very easy to please. He loves people and will move seamlessly from being a hard-working shooting companion to a fun-loving member of the family. Children are viewed as excellent playmates, and the gentle side of the Field's nature means that he is tolerant of babies and toddlers.

The male Field is a slightly bigger and heavier dog than the female. He is more likely to be at the upper limit of the weight range (around 50–55 pounds), and is slightly taller. In terms of temperament, there is not a marked difference between the sexes, although there is a belief that females tend to be slightly more tolerant and patient, which may be a consideration if you have small children.

Field Spaniels will live happily with other dogs as long as there is enough attention to go around. It is important to supervise interactions with cats in the early stages, but the Field is ready to live in harmony with felines and other small animals.

Trainability

The Field Spaniel is a clever dog who likes to please his human family, and so there are no real barriers to successful training. It is important to start at an early age and to be 100 percent consistent in everything you ask. This applies to housebreaking, enforcing house rules (e.g., whether your dog is allowed on the sofa or not), interactions with family members (e.g., always stopping the dog from jumping up), as well as training exercises. The Field will be as quick to learn bad habits as good habits, so the trick is to teach him the behavior that you want.

The breed is well known for its independent streak. This is a virtue in a working dog who has the initiative to go out in front of his handler to flush out game, but it can pose problems when your Field suddenly decides to do his own thing. The best plan is to make training sessions as much fun as possible so your Field will be stimulated by what he is doing. Provide lots of rewards—this can include verbal praise, stroking, games with a toy, and tasty treats—so your Field is strongly motivated to cooperate with you.

Do not make the mistake of being confrontational. You will discover that the Field's independent spirit can change to stubbornness, which is frustrating for the handler and nonproductive as far as the dog is concerned. Always play to your dog's strengths: the Field loves human company, and he thrives on being given things to do. With a little understanding, you will have no problems in establishing an excellent working partnership with your Field Spaniel.

Exercise

The Field Spaniel is an active, energetic dog. A program of varied exercise should be considered essential.

Start training at an early age so the ground rules are well established. Work on socialization as the Field Spaniel may be suspicious of unfamiliar situations.

The Field was bred to work in thick undergrowth, and he likes nothing better than having the chance to explore in this type of terrain. He is also a keen swimmer, and this provides an excellent form of exercise as long as you are confident that the conditions are 100 percent safe.

If you are short of time, you can still give your Field the chance to burn up energy by playing retrieve games with him. He will enjoy the free-running exercise, and he will also benefit from the interaction. Remember, the Field was bred for activity and for endurance, and so you will find that a long time passes before your Field runs out of energy.

As Fields are heavier in build than some of the other Spaniel breeds, take care not to overexercise your Field while he is still growing and his joints are vulnerable.

Grooming

The Field Spaniel has a moderately long, single coat, which is dense and water repellent. The coat is silky in texture, with feathering on the

The Field Spaniel is known for his independent streak, which is useful in a hunting dog but may need to be curbed in a companion dog.

ears, the chest, the underbody, the backs of the legs, and the underside of the tail.

The coat is relatively easy to keep in good order as long as you stick to regular grooming sessions so the coat does not start to mat and tangle.

- A bristle brush is the best grooming tool to use for a Field Spaniel. Work your way methodically through the coat, starting at the front and working along the body. To get at the underbody, you will need to ask your Field to lie on his side. With training, he might even agree to roll onto his back, which will make the job easier.
- Repeat the process with a comb, paying particular attention to the feathering. If you come across any mats or tangles, they will need to be teased out gently.
- The Field Spaniel's ears are his crowning glory, so make sure the hair is tangle free, and check behind the ears where mats may form.

- If you plan to show your Field Spaniel, he will need a little scissoring to maintain a good outline. The areas to be trimmed are the back legs (from hocks to the ground), the underside of the tail, around the paws and between the pads, and the upper one-third of the outer ear to allow the ears to lie flat, framing the head.
- Many exhibitors will also use finger and thumb or a stripping knife to pluck hair around the dome of the head, at the set on of the ears, and at the front of the neck for a clean outline. In the United States, clippers are sometimes used, but this is frowned upon in the U.K.
- For the companion dog, the only trimming that is required is around the paws, and particularly between the pads. The Field Spaniel has large webbed feet, and he will be very uncomfortable if the hair grows too long or becomes matted.

Health Concerns

The Field Spaniel is a hardy breed, and there are few inherited conditions of significance.

- **Hip dysplasia:** This is probably the most common of inherited diseases in Field Spaniels, and so all breeding stock should be hip tested. The OFA ranks Field Spaniels 40th in its breed listing, showing an incidence of hip dysplasia of 18.6 percent for dogs tested from 1974 to the present day (see page 22).
- **Progressive retinal atrophy:** This is occasionally seen, and again, breeding stock should be eye tested (see page 23).
- **Thyroid disease:** This is a condition when the thyroid malfunctions, resulting in reduced

output. The signs are hair loss, lethargy, and a tendency to gain weight.

- **Ectropion:** Not a major problem in the breed, but check the incidence in previous generations (see page 23).
- **Patellar luxation:** Only very occasionally seen (see page 22).

NEW CHALLENGES

The Field Spaniel was bred primarily as a sporting companion. Over a period of time, he has evolved into being a versatile dog who can adapt himself to a number of different challenges.

Hunting

Working instinct is strong in all Field Spaniels, and with the correct training, he is an excellent hunter. The Field's specialty is working in dense cover. By using his excellent sense of smell, he quarters the ground methodically, moving with a long, unhurried stride, and will then flush out game—generally pheasants and quail (plus chukars in the United States). He has a soft mouth and will retrieve the game to hand. The Field is an excellent swimmer and is happy retrieving from water.

An invaluable member of informal hunting expeditions, the Field Spaniel can also be trained to compete in field and water tests.

Obedience

Bright, intelligent, and quick to learn, the Field Spaniel has the ability to compete in obedience, and a number have proved to be highly successful. It is important to bear in mind the Field's independent streak. He likes to think for himself—and this may not always be desirable.

However, if you work hard on motivation, the Field will be happy to work with you.

Agility

The Field Spaniel may not be as fast as a Border Collie, but he can still move at speed on an agility course. The Field enjoys the fun of this sport, and his bold nature means that he is ready to work out in front of his handler—rather than staying close by the handler's side—which can prove advantageous in timed competitions.

Tracking

Tracking comes naturally to the Field, who was bred to work with his nose. The terrain causes no problems, as the Field is ready to work in open landscapes or in thick cover. His desire to please his handler helps to create many winning partnerships in tracking tests.

The Field Spaniel works methodically to flush out game and uses his soft mouth to retrieve.

Showing

The Field Spaniel cuts a fine figure in the show ring. Although his coat requires attention, it is not as labor intensive as some long-coated breeds. Training for the ring should start at an early age, but the Field is quick to catch on to what is required and he conducts himself very well.

Therapy Dogs

Because the Field Spaniel is not strong in numbers, there are only a few who work as therapy dogs. In fact, the breed is ideally suited to this work. The Field Spaniel is very sensitive, and is unusually docile. He has the ability to tune into situations and can be gentle or full of impish good humor, as the occasion demands.

CHAMPION CALVIN

Shannon T. Rodgers, from Iowa, is the proud owner of Calvin (Ch. U-CD UAG-I Maplesugar Calvin CD NA CGC TDIA), a truly versatile Field Spaniel who competes in a variety of canine activities. Here, Shannon describes some of her and Calvin's experiences in tracking and rally-o.

"Calvin is my first 'official' dog. I researched the different breeds and settled on Field Spaniels because I loved their performance abilities and breed characteristics. I am constantly surprised at the breed's incredible character. I enjoy a naturally intuitive canine companion who enjoys training and trying new things. As our breed standard states, Field Spaniels are a 'combination of beauty and utility,' and Calvin demonstrates those qualities in our activities.

"Calvin came to me when he was four years old. His breeder wanted to place him in a 'performance home' where he would have a job to do once finishing his conformation career. When I began looking for a dog, I made it clear that I wanted to become involved in obedience, agility, tracking, and therapy work. I'm really glad that Calvin's breeder, Cheryl Benedict, thought Calvin and I would form an ideal partnership.

"I love training with Calvin, especially in several different disciplines. You learn something from each of them, honing a wide variety of skills, including precision, usefulness, scent, speed, agility, teamwork, problem solving, and, most importantly, the bond between you and your dog."

FOLLOWING THE SCENT

"Tracking is a unique sport involving the dog's amazing scent abilities. It's a wonderful activity that is ideal for Field Spaniels. They have an affinity for working in the outdoors. Their bodies and feet are naturally suited for covering the ground efficiently and tirelessly, and they have superb noses. You can't expect those natural instincts not to show; you are far better off cultivating them!

"Initially, we started with basic tracks that were easy to follow and worked up to more demanding tracks. During training, we normally follow a human scent trail that leads to a glove or wallet. When you plot the track, you leave a scent as you crush vegetation and turn corners, and it is this combination of human scent in that environment that the dog follows. As dog and handler become more skilled, the tracks are made more difficult—they can be aged, crossed with tracks of a different scent, or involve several different articles on different terrain.

"When you first start tracking, you find yourself learning from the dog's instinct. I had to learn how to read Calvin and to communicate effectively with him during training. Tracking certainly teaches you to trust your dog! You quickly discover that 'the nose knows!' I can only chuckle when Calvin tries to tell me adamantly something that I just should have listened to him in the first place. I've found that working with a tracking 'training buddy' is a big help in learning to understand when your dog was *on* track when you thought he was *off*.

"Tracking is special to me. I love to watch the instinct and beauty Calvin possesses when he is scenting. Sometimes, witnessing the sheer canine joy of running over the grass or capturing a toy makes me laugh. Tracking is also very special for Calvin. It is a time for him to sniff and to reap the benefits of outdoor exercise and joyous praise!"

RALLY-O
Recently, Calvin and I have taken up rally-o. This is a form of obedience but with the emphasis on communication and teamwork over a designed course. It does not require the same precision as competition obedience. A course comprises several 'stations' each with a sign that indicates the next command, such as perform a sit or turn 270 degrees and walk to heel. At the higher levels, the exercises become more difficult, involving low jumps and food distractions.

Calvin and Shannon: The Field Spaniel is an intelligent dog and will make his mark in many of the sporting disciplines.

"Rally-o is fun because it is never routine. You can talk to your dog the whole time, and new courses keep it fresh and challenging. You see all breeds and levels of ability getting involved, from rank beginners stepping into the ring for the first time to seasoned handlers just having fun with a veteran obedience dog. It is meant to be a positive venue open to many levels of experience.

"Calvin particularly enjoys rally-o because he likes the constant feedback and encouragement he receives, as opposed to the single commands or signals he receives in traditional obedience. During any type of training, Calvin likes to remind me that we are doing this for fun. He has a sense of humor, and rally-o allows his individual personality to come out.

"Calvin is my lovely brown boy. I adore his sense of humor and zest for life. We are looking forward to many more years of fun and learning together."

CHAPTER NINE

THE IRISH WATER SPANIEL

The tallest of the Spaniel breeds, the Irish Water Spaniel is also big on personality. Playful and mischievous, he has a clownish sense of humor, which typifies his zest for life. He may not be classically handsome, but few can resist his rugged charm or his bright, quizzical gaze.

Bred to retrieve from water, the Irish Water Spaniel is bold and tireless and thinks nothing of breaking through ice to retrieve waterfowl or finding his way through thick brambles when he is working on the land. An intelligent, quick-thinking dog, the Irish Water Spaniel is also loving and affectionate. He makes an excellent companion for those who favor an active lifestyle.

He is well balanced and athletic in build, and despite his height, he does not give an impression of legginess. He is smart and upstanding and is capable of both strength and endurance. The liver-colored coat, covered in crisp ringlets, is the outstanding feature of the breed. The topknot—a mass of loose curls—makes a striking contrast with the smooth face, as does the short, smooth rat tail, which stands out against the curly coated body.

This has always been a breed for specialists, and numbers working in the field and being exhibited in the show ring are relatively small. However, those who own the breed are generally smitten for life.

BREED HISTORY

Water-retrieving Spaniels have ancient roots, dating back to Roman times. Carvings that show dogs with a strong resemblance to the Irish Water Spaniel have been found in Roman ruins in Europe. However, the documented history of the breed starts in southern Ireland in the 1100s, with references to dogs living by the River Shannon. They were variously known as Shannon Spaniels, Rat-Tail Spaniels, Whip-Tail Spaniels, and Irish Water Spaniels. It is impossible to work out which breeds were used to create this Irish water retriever, but it is thought that the Afghan Hound (who has a

A tough, working dog, the Irish Water Spaniel's reputation spread to the United States.

similar high-domed head and proud head carriage) and the Poodle (who has a curly coat, providing perfect protection in the water) may well have played a significant role.

Two types of water Spaniel eventually emerged in Ireland. The northern variety was liver colored with white markings. It had short ears and a curly coat and was similar to the English Water Spaniel. In the south, the Water Spaniel was solid liver and had long, feathered ears and a tight, curly coat.

McCarthy's Breed

In the early 1800s, a keen sportsman called Justin McCarthy established his own kennel of Water Spaniels in Dublin. They were based on the southern variety, but he may well have selectively bred with northern dogs. His dogs were greatly admired for their looks and for their working ability, and over a period of time, he developed a uniformity of type. Dogs from his breeding were known as "McCarthy's breed."

The turning point came in 1834 with the birth of a dog called Boatswain. He grew up to be an impressive dog—just the type that McCarthy was striving for—and he went on to become a hugely influential stud dog. He is considered by many to be the original sire of the breed. It is remarkable that the Irish Water Spaniels of today bear a striking resemblance to their founding father.

It was not long before news of these tough working dogs, with their distinctive liver-colored curly coats, spread outside Ireland. Fanciers in England took up the breed, and classes for Irish Water Spaniels were scheduled at the Birmingham Show in 1862. In the United States, there was considerable interest in the breed's working ability. A dog that was big and strong enough to retrieve ducks and geese, and could also withstand cold water, sounded like the ideal shooting companion. A number of Irish Water Spaniels were imported, and the breed soon became the popular choice of wildfowl hunters. By 1875, it was the third most popular sporting dog in the United States.

However, their popularity was to be short-lived. Labrador Retrievers and Golden Retrievers were tried out by sportsmen, and they were found to be ideal all-around workers. They were easier to train, more docile, and their coats were simpler to maintain. The Irish Water Spaniel retained its own specialist following, but numbers fell dramatically.

THE IRISH WATER SPANIEL TODAY

This is a breed that has never been prey to the whims of fashion. Over the years, the Irish Water Spaniel has remained very true to its original type. It is small in numbers in both the U.K. and the U.S. It is currently ranked 135th in the American Kennel Club breed listings, with registrations of 116 a year. In the U.K., it is 121st, with 121 registrations a year.

Clearly a dog for the specialist, devotees of the Irish Water Spaniel are determined that the dogs produced are sound and healthy, with good working ability, and typical specimens of this highly distinctive breed. Cooperation between breeders in the U.K., Scandinavia, and the United States has resulted in a first-class gene pool, and the future of the breed looks increasingly bright.

Both the American Kennel Club and the Kennel Club in the U.K. have drawn up their own breed standards, but there is little difference in their descriptions of the ideal Irish Water Spaniel.

General Appearance
A smart, upstanding, strongly built sporting dog.

Breed Characteristics
A versatile gundog that combines great intelligence with rugged endurance and a bold, dashing eagerness of temperament. Used for all types of shooting, particularly wildfowling.

Temperament
Alert and inquisitive, the Irish Water Spaniel is initially aloof and reserved with strangers but is staunch and affectionate with an endearing sense of humor and a stable disposition.

Head
A good-sized head, the skull is high in dome; it is of good length and width, allowing adequate

The breed's swimming ability is legendary. The dense, curly coat protects the dog in icy temperatures, and water drips off as soon as he emerges from the water.

brain capacity. The muzzle is long and square with a gradual stop. The face is smooth and cleanly chiseled. The nose is well developed and dark liver in color.

Eyes
Comparatively small (according to the British standard) or medium in size (according to the American standard), the eyes are almond shaped. The color is medium hazel to dark brown, and the expression is intelligent, keenly alert, direct, and quizzical.

Ears
Long, oval in shape, and set on low, hanging close to the cheeks. The ear leather should reach to the end of the nose. Abundantly covered in long curls, which extend 2–3 inches (5–8 cm) below the tips of the leathers.

Mouth
The jaws and teeth are strong, meeting in a

scissor bite (the upper teeth closely overlapping the lower teeth) and set square to the jaw.

Neck

The neck is long, arching, and muscular, set strongly into the shoulders. It is long enough to carry the head well above the level of the back.

Forequarters

The front assembly gives an impression of strength without heaviness. The shoulders are powerful and sloping. The chest is deep, with reasonable width and curvature between the front legs. The elbows are set close, and the legs are straight and well boned.

Body

The body is of medium length. The ribs are carried well back and are so well sprung as to give a barrel shape. The back is short, broad, and level, and the loins are wide and muscular.

Hindquarters

Sound hinquarters are of great importance to provide swimming power and drive. They should be muscular and as high as or slightly higher than the shoulders, with well-developed thighs. The hips are wide, the stifles are moderately bent, and the hocks are low set.

Feet

Large, round, and spreading, they are well covered with hair both over and between the toes.

Tail

The "rat tail" is a feature of the breed. It is low set, below the level of the back. It is straight and short, not reaching to the hock joint, and thick at the root, tapering to a fine point. Tight curls cover the root of the tail, going down 3–4 inches /7.5–10 cm (British standard) 2–3 inches/5–7.5 cm (American standard) and then stop abruptly. The rest of the tail is covered in short, straight, fine hairs.

The Irish Water Spaniel is a strongly built sporting dog with a look of rugged endurance.

The face is smooth and cleanly chiseled.

Movement

The Irish Water Spaniel moves freely and soundly, showing reach and drive. The British standard notes a characteristic rolling motion, accentuated by the barrel-shaped rib cage.

Coat

A double coat is of vital importance to protect the dog when working. The body is covered with dense, tight, crisp ringlets, which have a naturally oily texture and is free from wooliness. The forelegs are covered down to the feet with abundant curls or waves, which are shorter in front. Below the hocks, the hind legs should be smooth in front with curls behind, going down to the feet.

The skull has long curls, making a pronounced topknot, and the ears have long, twisted curls. The neck has curls like the rest of the body. The neck is smooth, forming a V-shaped patch from the back of the lower jaw to the breastbone. The muzzle and foreface are also smooth coated.

Color

Solid liver. The British standard notes that the color should be rich and dark with a purplish tint—known as puce liver—which is peculiar to the breed.

Size

- **British standard:** Males 21–23 inches (53–58 cm), females 20–22 inches (51–56 cm).
- **American standard:** Males 22–24 inches (56–61 cm), weight 55–65 pounds (25–29.5 kg). Females 21–23 inches (53–58 cm), weight 45–58 pounds (20.5–26.3 kg).

LIVING WITH AN IRISH WATER SPANIEL

Big, strong, and active, the Irish Water Spaniel is a breed that takes some looking after. Anyone attracted to the breed should examine the pros and cons before taking the plunge into ownership.

Family Situation

This is a breed that is much better suited to country living than to an urban setting. It would be a daunting task to attempt to provide for the exercise needs of this breed without easy access to free-running areas.

The Irish Water Spaniel is an excellent family dog, as he tends to see his whole family as one special person, rather than bonding with an individual. He gets on well with children—particularly older children—but he should always be treated with respect. This is a strong dog who will not appreciate being teased and plagued by unruly toddlers. Loving and affectionate with his family, the Irish Water

This breed has a dashing eagerness of temperament and is not well suited to the constraints of urban living.

With positive training, the Irish Water Spaniel is a cooperative companion and will be more than ready to have a go at any of the canine sports.

Spaniel is often reserved with strangers, or he may show complete indifference, being far more interested in his own people.

The male is bigger than the female, and he can be a little more headstrong. If you are new to the breed, it is probably better to opt for a female. Males are not always keen on sharing their home with another male dog, and most Irish Water Spaniels prefer being the one, special dog in the family.

Trainability

The Irish Water Spaniel is a clever dog, and he has proved this in many of the canine disciplines, but he is not the easiest to train. Bred to work in demanding conditions, he is mentally and physically tough, and this makes him strong-minded and independent. It is very

important to start training at an early age so that the dog understands his place in the family and sees the point of cooperating.

Motivation is the key to training, and you will need to find out what works for your Irish Water Spaniel. It may be food, or he may focus on a special training toy. Whatever you choose, make sure your dog sees the treat or the toy as a reward he really *wants* to work for. The Irish Water Spaniel has a reputation for being stubborn, but in most cases, this is the result of unimaginative training. If you are having problems with an exercise, think of another way to train it, or work on something you know your dog likes to do rather than becoming involved in a nonproductive confrontation.

All owners of Irish Water Spaniels comment on the breed's impish sense of humor. You may well find that your dog's idea of fun is playing tricks on you! You can also train him to perform tricks for you, and he will relish the opportunity to show off in front of his beloved family.

Exercise

There is no better breed to choose if you have an active lifestyle. The Irish Water Spaniel is full of energy; he is lively and inquisitive and loves to run and explore. If you cannot provide a program of varied and extensive exercise, you would be better off choosing a more sedate breed.

Bred to retrieve from water, the Irish Water Spaniel is an exceptional swimmer and will seize on any opportunity to get wet. If you have access to a safe stretch of water, you will have endless entertainment playing retrieve games with your dog.

The Irish Water Spaniel is very playful. You can burn up some of his excess energy by inventing games for him—such as finding a hidden toy—which will also exercise his brain.

Grooming

The Irish Water Spaniel's curly coat is his most distinctive feature and is often what first attracts new owners to the breed. It does not shed as profusely as other types of coat, and so allergy sufferers may well be able to tolerate living with an Irish Water Spaniel. The coat is not difficult to care for, but regular grooming sessions—at least twice weekly—are essential.

- A bristle brush can be used for routine grooming. A hound glove is useful for getting rid of dead hair.
- The coat sheds slightly throughout the year, but twice yearly (in the spring and the autumn) there is a more complete shed. At this time, the coat must be combed (with a wide-toothed comb) or raked out thoroughly. The dead hairs tend to get trapped in other hairs (rather than falling out) and will form into mats (known as dust bunnies) or cords unless they are combed out.
- Special attention must be paid to cleaning ears and trimming excess hair from inside them.
- The coat will need trimming with scissors to neaten the appearance. This can be done every couple of months or more often if you are showing your dog. Generally, scissoring should follow the natural lines of the body, making sure the coat is not trimmed too short. A useful tip is to spray the coat with rainwater, which enhances the tight, crisp curls.

The American breed standard states that dogs can be shown in natural coat or trimmed, but no dog should be groomed or trimmed so excessively as to obscure the curl or texture of the coat. There is a tendency to "overproduce" the Irish Water Spaniel in the show ring, and true devotees are concerned that the breed's rugged charm will be lost in the interest of presentation.

Health Concerns

The tall, athletic Irish Water Spaniel is one of the most hardy of the Spaniel breeds and remains relatively free from inherited health problems. Check out the following:

- **Hip dysplasia:** Ranked 66th by the OFA in terms of incidence of the condition, 13 percent of dogs assessed were found to be dysplastic. All breeding stock should be tested (see page 22).

The show dog should look neat and smart—but he should not lose his rugged good looks.

Ch. O'rlook's Brown Sugar makes agility look easy. The breed's exuberant nature comes to the fore in this discipline.

- **Skin conditions:** Generally, chocolate and liver-colored dogs are more likely to be affected by skin conditions and allergies, so it is important to groom your dog regularly and to keep a close check on his coat and skin.
- **Ear infections:** These seem to plague some Irish Water Spaniels, so keep a close check on the ears (see above).

NEW CHALLENGES

As a breed, the Irish Water Spaniel is far from common, and so it is rare to see him in competition. With dedicated training, though, he is capable of major achievements.

Hunting

The Irish Water Spaniel is the only Spaniel that is classified as a retriever with the American Kennel Club. This allows him to compete in field trials and hunting tests designed for retrievers.

There is no doubt that the Irish Water Spaniel is a bold and fearless retriever, working with a zeal that is unparalleled. He is big enough to retrieve a bird as large as a Canadian goose, and he will think nothing of swimming through icy waters or plunging through boggy marshland to reach his quarry. On the land, the Irish Water

Spaniel is a determined hunter, following a trail through the thickest cover. Sportsmen also comment on the breed's exceptional vision. He is able to see moving objects from a great distance, and this is invaluable when marking game.

The breed's thick, curly coat acts as excellent protection—after a dozen retrieves, his skin will generally be dry. However, some sportsmen trim the coat, as it attracts burrs, which can be a menace.

Obedience

Bred to work with a fair degree of independence, the Irish Water Spaniel does not take naturally to the close precision demanded in obedience competition. He is easily bored by repetition. If you take on the challenge of competitive obedience, you will need to work at making it varied and stimulating.

Interestingly, the breed has been chosen by some canine freestyle competitors. The Irish Water Spaniel's flamboyant personality seems to suit this discipline.

Agility

Fast, fearless, and athletic, the Irish Water Spaniel thoroughly enjoys agility training, and it is an excellent way of using up his abundant energy. Control is all-important, and your dog must learn the basics of obedience before competing in this discipline.

Tracking

The breed's working capabilities remain very strong, and tracking comes easily to the Irish Water Spaniel. He is determined, with great endurance, and will rarely give up on a trail.

Showing

The Irish Water Spaniel can make an impressive show dog, but you need to work with a dog who has a natural air of showmanship and does not mind being handled. Notable wins for the breed include Best in Show at the prestigious Westminster Show in 1979 and Sporting Group wins, again at Westminster, in 1990 and 1991.

Therapy Dogs

The Irish Water Spaniel tends to be wary of strangers. Although he is a very loving dog within his own family circle, the task of therapy work may not always suit him.

MADCAP MOVES

Betty Wathne, of Maryland, has been practicing freestyle performances with her Irish Water Spaniels for nearly 15 years, since the sport's early days. Here, Betty describes the appeal of freestyle and why it is so enjoyable for Irish Water Spaniels and their owners.

"I became interested in Irish Water Spaniels because I wanted a dog that could do more than 'just' conformation or 'just' obedience. I wanted something versatile and a bit different, which would be fun to train. I haven't been disappointed in my expectations! Irishers are great—I love their ability to exhibit enough drive and enthusiasm for any dog sport or activity and yet also be a quiet companion around the house.

"I was fortunate that my first Irish Water Spaniel was a fantastic dog to work, live, and compete with. Gallant (Ch. Donnybrook Madcap Gallantry UD JH WC) was a joy, and I'm delighted that all my other dogs are descended from him and share some of his spark and dashing temperament. I now have four Irish Water Spaniels: Blaze (Ch. Castlehill's

Blazing Madcap UD NA, a 14-year-old bitch), Valor (Ch. Beaufield's Valiant Madcap CDX JH WC, the 11-year-old half-brother of Blaze), True (BISS Ch. Madcap's Brilliant Virtue CD, Blaze's daughter), and Gabriel (Ch. Madcap's If My Heart Had Wings, True's son). They all compete in freestyle, as well as other disciplines, such as obedience and conformation. Gabriel is the baby of the pack, new to the performance ring.

"When Blaze was a youngster, I encouraged her to develop a stylized movement while heeling. Thanks to her athleticism, willing mind, and good structure, she developed a heeling style with a floating, suspended trot that was lovely and lilting all on its own. Then I heard about a new sport—choreographing heelwork to music—and I decided that it was an ideal opportunity to show off Blaze's beautiful technique.

"When I first became involved in freestyle, I was completely clueless about choreography. A lady called Jan Tenille helped me enormously by choreographing my first program. Blaze and I graduated quickly to performing demonstrations

Continued on page 104

Continued from page 103

of that program at a regional obedience competition and at the first AKC Obedience Invitational. I also performed at the Irish Water Spaniel Club of America National Specialty, and that began a tradition of freestyle demonstrations at the specialties—it's such fun to watch that people can't get enough! I've also done demonstrations at kennel clubs, horse shows, and society fundraisers. There are now a number of IWS trainers performing at specialty shows, showing how versatile these dogs are and how quickly they adapt to freestyle. They truly want to be there and they love to work, so their personalities really shine through.

"Every time we perform, I get totally carried away by my dogs' enjoyment. It is an honor to step in the ring with them. I shall never forget my first performance with Blaze. I have always been struck by her grace, but I never expected the entire audience to feel the same way. It was an incredibly moving experience.

"There are so many special things about freestyle. Nothing can compare to the pleasure of finding a piece of music that brings out a dog's character and complements its movement. It's also interesting to watch the dogs develop over time. When I first started performing with Valor, we used to choreograph to bouncy rock-and-roll songs. For a while after that, swing music suited him best. Then we moved on to magnificent orchestral pieces, later followed by rock ballads. This year will see Valor's farewell demonstration, and we will be performing to a quiet, slow-paced song. Valor has so much experience, and his personality so

much presence, that the program will be embodied with drama and emotion.

"In 2003, I was involved in a very special program. Six retired obedience-titled Irishers, all breed champions ranging from 10 to $13\frac{1}{2}$, performed a group routine. We chose a song that celebrated the time we have left with our treasured veterans. Some of the dogs were a bit stiff, but it was clear how much every single one of them enjoyed being out there. Blaze, the oldest, had a wonderful time. Stepping back into the ring with her, years after her retirement, was a real gift. I don't think there was a dry eye in the house!

"Despite the fact that some of my dogs are now retired, or about to be, I plan to continue with freestyle on a demonstration level, bringing up younger dogs. I may even try some competition again, as the idea of competing internationally is very appealing to me. Whichever path I follow, I know that it will be intensely enjoyable and rewarding for me and for my wonderful dogs."

Betty enjoys performing with her dogs Valor (Ch. Beaufield's Valiant Madcap CDX JH WC) and True (Ch. Madcap's Brilliant Virtue CD).

CHAPTER TEN

THE SUSSEX SPANIEL

The massively built Sussex Spaniel, with his glorious golden liver color, has had a checkered history. Although small in numbers, the breed has a loyal band of supporters who appreciate his qualities as a determined hunting dog and as a kindly and loyal companion.

Bred in the county of Sussex in England, the Sussex Spaniel was developed to suit local hunting conditions on the large country estates. Long and low in build, the Sussex Spaniel could cope with the heavy clay soil and thick cover of the region. His excellent sense of smell was invaluable for locating quarry, and his habit of "giving tongue" prior to flushing was an asset for sportsmen following behind on foot.

The Sussex Spaniel is an energetic worker, but he moves at a slower pace than most of the other Spaniel breeds. He can also be something of a couch potato if nothing much is happening. Calm and steady in temperament, he is a loving companion and can be quite protective of his home.

The hallmark of the breed is its golden liver color, which is quite distinct from the liver color seen in other Sporting Spaniels, such as the Field Spaniel or the Irish Water Spaniel. The Sussex Spaniel has a low-set body, with a deep chest and powerful hindquarters. He has a rolling gait, which is another characteristic of the breed. The head is large and wide, with a heavy, frowning brow, which gives the dog a somber, serious expression.

Warm and friendly, the Sussex Spaniel is not as needy as some of the other Spaniel breeds. However, he has a constancy, coupled with a mischievous streak, which makes him a most endearing companion.

BREED HISTORY

The Sussex Spaniel is very much a local dog, developed in the English county of Sussex in the 1800s and then gradually becoming more widespread as its reputation became established. It is thought that the Tweed Water Spaniel, and possibly a hound, played a part in the makeup

Ch. Stonecroft Cosenza JH, WD,
CGC, owned by Ann McGloon.
Photo: Creative Indulgence.

of the breed. However, type was cemented by the Rosehill Park Kennel in Sussex, which was set up in 1795 by Augustus Elliot Fuller. He bred his own strain of Spaniels specifically for hunting and was ably assisted by his kennel manager, Albert Reif. In those early days, interbreeding with the Field Spaniel was not uncommon. It is widely accepted that it was the Rosehill breeding program that developed the golden liver color, which is so much a characteristic of the Sussex Spaniel.

The Sussex Spaniel was exhibited at dog shows in 1862 and attracted moderate interest. News of the breed spread to the U.S., and a number of dogs were imported in the late 1800s. In fact, the Sussex Spaniel was the fifth breed to be recognized by the American Kennel Club. However, sportsmen in the U.S. generally wanted a faster dog, and the Sussex Spaniel remained small in numbers. It was not faring much better in the U.K., as the breed's tendency to vocalize when hunting was proving a drawback in field trials. However, there were a number of dedicated breeders in the U.K. who were determined to keep the breed alive.

The Sussex Spaniel has never really taken off as a show dog. However, his working abilities and his sound, kindly disposition were appreciated, and the breed was kept going by a small but select band of enthusiasts, most particularly Moses Woolland and Campbell Newington. Unfortunately, disaster struck with the outbreak of the Second World War. The numbers of Sussex Spaniels fell so dramatically that the breed was close to extinction.

It is entirely due to the sacrifices made by Joyce Freer of the Fourclovers Kennel that the

Small in numbers, the Sussex Spaniel has a dedicated band of enthusiasts.

© Creative Indulgence

breed survived. She had been breeding Sussex Spaniels since the 1920s, and she was determined to save her beloved breed. Conditions were so hard that this sometimes meant going without food herself in order to feed her dogs. By the end of the war, eight dogs survived—the last remaining Sussex Spaniels in the U.K.

Because the gene pool was so small, it was necessary to introduce new bloodlines to ensure the breed's future. In the 1950s, crosses were made with the Clumber Spaniel and also with the English Springer Spaniel. Slowly, numbers built up again, and the Sussex Spaniel's future was assured.

THE SUSSEX SPANIEL TODAY

The survival of the Sussex Spaniel was little short of miraculous, and although the breed is small in numbers, the quality of dogs is excellent. The breed is currently ranked 137th by the AKC—the least popular of the Sporting Spaniels—with just over 100 registrations a year. In the U.K., the Sussex Spaniel is also the least

The Sussex is a massive dog, but he should still appear capable of doing a day's work on the field.

popular of the Spaniels in the Gundog Group, with a ranking of 147th and 68 registrations a year. There are small gains in terms of show ring entries, and breed enthusiasts work hard to ensure that the Sussex Spaniel retains his working capabilities. However, this is likely to remain a breed for the connoisseur.

The AKC and the Kennel Club in the U.K. both have their own breed standards, which describe the perfect Sussex Spaniel.

General Appearance

A massive, strongly built dog who is active and energetic, his outline is rectangular, as the Sussex Spaniel is longer in body than he is tall.

Breed Characteristics

A natural worker, he gives tongue (vocalizes) when working in thick cover. The distinctive rolling gait is unique to the breed, as is the rich golden liver color.

Temperament

Despite his somber and serious expression, the Sussex Spaniel has a kindly and tractable disposition. He is friendly and cheerful—any sign of aggression is highly undesirable.

Head

The skull is wide with a moderate curve from ear to ear; there is an indentation in the middle and a pronounced stop. The brows are heavy and frowning, and the occiput is decided but not pointed. The head is well balanced, giving an impression of heaviness without dullness. The muzzle is approximately 3 inches (7.5 cm) long and square in profile. The nostrils are well developed and liver colored.

Eyes

Fairly large and hazel in color, with a soft, languishing expression, the eyes should not show much haw.

Ears

The ears are thick, fairly large, and lobe shaped. They are set moderately low, just above eye level, and lie close to the skull.

Mouth

Strong jaws with a scissor bite (upper teeth closely overlapping the lower teeth).

Neck

The neck is strong, muscular, and slightly arched. Both the American and the British standards agree that the head is not carried much above the level of the back, but the American standard states that the neck is "rather short," whereas the British standard calls for a "long" neck.

Forequarters

The shoulders are sloping and muscular. The legs are set well under the dog, and they are short, strong, and heavily boned. The pasterns are short and strong. The American standard allows for both a straight and bowed construction of the forelegs.

Body

The chest is deep and well developed but should not be too round or too wide. The topline is level, and both the back and the loin are well developed and muscular in width and depth. The whole body is strong and level, and there should be no sign of waistline from withers to hips.

Hindquarters

The thighs are strongly boned and muscular, the hocks are large and strong, and the legs are short and strong, with good bone. The hind legs should not appear shorter than the forelegs or be overangulated.

Feet

The feet are large, round, and well padded with hair growing between the toes. The American standard asks for "short hair," but it should be sufficiently long to cover the nails; the British standard states that the feet should be "well feathered" between the toes.

Tail

The tail is set on low and is never carried above the level of the back. Customarily docked to a length of 5–7 inches (12.75–17.75 cm), the tail action is lively.

Movement

The round, deep, wide chest; the short legs; and long body produces a distinctive rolling gait. The movement is deliberate, never clumsy, with perfect coordination between the front and hind legs.

Coat

The body coat is abundant and flat, with no tendency to curl. The undercoat should be sufficient to provide protection against the weather. The ears are covered with soft, wavy hair; the forequarters and hindquarters are moderately well feathered. The tail is thickly clothed with hair—"but not feathered" according to the British standard, or "with

The rich, golden liver coat is unique to the breed.

moderately long feather" according to the American standard.

Color
Rich golden liver, the hair shading to golden at the tip but gold should predominate. Dark liver or puce is undesirable and is considered a major fault according to the American standard.

Size
- **American standard:** 13–15 inches (33–38 cm) at the shoulder; weight 35–45 pounds (15.8–20.4 kg).
- **British standard:** 15–16 inches (38–41 cm); weight approximately 50 pounds (23 kg).

LIVING WITH A SUSSEX SPANIEL
The Sussex Spaniel is a keen hunter, but he is also an adaptable type and can fit in with a number of different lifestyles. He has a strong

Generally, the Sussex Spaniel likes to be the sole dog in a family—but there are exceptions to the rule.

© Sally McCully

character, and this should be considered when deciding if this is the right Spaniel breed for you.

Family Situation
Long, low set, and massively built, the Sussex Spaniel does not have the exuberance of some of the other Spaniel breeds, but he certainly makes his presence felt. He loves his family and gets on well with children if he has been brought up with them. He sees his role as being in the center of family life, and it is his job to protect his home and his family.

As a result, the Sussex Spaniel can be quite a vocal watchdog as he warns of the approach of strangers. He is reserved with people he does not know and will not accept children outside the family taking liberties with him. With careful supervision, he may tolerate cats and other small animals, but this should not be taken for granted. Some Sussex Spaniels have too strong a hunting instinct to be able to live in harmony with potential "game."

Generally speaking, Sussex Spaniels prefer to be the sole dog in the family, enjoying all the attention that comes their way. They certainly see strange dogs as a threat—particularly if they are invited into the house—so this is a situation that is best avoided.

This breed is relatively easy to care for in limited space. He will adapt to urban living as long as his exercise needs are cared for.

Trainability
The Sussex Spaniel's personality is generally cheerful, friendly, and easygoing, and he loves being with people. All these can be considered plus points when it comes to training as the

Sussex is keen to be an integral part of family life. He has a kindly and tractable disposition, and he will see the point in a general level of cooperation, particularly if there are rewards offered. It is important to find out what your Sussex rates as a reward that is worth working for, as there appears to be no set pattern within the breed. Some are great foodies, others focus on a favorite toy, and some are content with lots of verbal praise.

The Sussex Spaniel appears to take life in stride, but he does have a sensitive side. In the face of harsh handling or punishment, he will almost literally fall apart and will be incapable of giving the correct response until he has gotten back on an even keel. He can also be stubborn, particularly if he does not understand what is required, and he is a master at digging in his heels. The experienced Sussex owner does not let either of these situations arise. There is no point in provoking conflicts or making a dog insecure and unhappy simply because you are making too many demands.

Adapt your training to suit your dog and then you will enjoy the benefits of a close and harmonious relationship. If your Sussex trusts you not to pressure him, he will become a willing and cooperative companion.

Exercise

The Sussex was bred to be a steady, methodical worker, and he does not have the lightning pace of some of the other Spaniel breeds. However, this does not mean that his exercise needs are minimal. He is an active and energetic dog, and he relishes the opportunity to use his excellent sense of smell. There is nothing your Sussex will

The Sussex has a sensitive side to his nature and will resent harsh handling.

The Sussex thrives on interesting outings.

Keen to work, the Sussex also enjoys his down time.

© Sally McCully

enjoy more than a long country ramble where he has the chance to go off lead and investigate all the fascinating scents. If you live in a city, you will need to work at making your dog's exercise routine as varied and interesting as possible.

Most Sussex Spaniels are good swimmers, and this constitutes a useful form of exercise. Unlike the other Spaniel breeds, the Sussex is not a natural retriever, but he can be taught with a little patience.

This is not a great breed if you are house-proud, as mud seems to stick to their coats. The Sussex seems to be fairly careless about his own appearance and will be happy to bring all mud and debris he has collected home with him.

Grooming

The stunning, rich, golden liver coat is the outstanding feature of the breed, and with regular grooming (twice weekly), you can maintain the beautiful sheen of the coat. If you plan to show your Sussex in the ring, he will need a little more attention.

- Use a bristle brush or a slicker brush, and groom your dog thoroughly head to tail.
- Pay particular attention to the feathered parts of the body. The soft wavy hair on the ears mats very easily. The other area where mats form readily are in the "armpit" and groin area.
- After brushing the coat, use a wide-toothed comb, teasing out any mats or tangles in the feathering. It may help if you use a grooming spray, which makes grooming easier and prevents the hair from breaking.
- Use scissors to trim hair on the inside of the ears and on the underside of the feet between the pads. Remember, the hair on the feet should be left long enough to cover the nails.
- Do not be tempted to bath your Sussex too often. Bathing destroys the natural oils of the coat. If it is done too frequently, your dog's coat will become dull and lose its bright color. If your Sussex has rolled in something and you have no option other than to bathe him, use plain water only.
- In the show ring, the Sussex Spaniel is neatened up by plucking out dead hair with finger and thumb. The job is made easier if you use rubber thimbles. The areas that need attention are the top of the head, the back, the flanks, and the hindquarters.

The American breed standard states, "No trimming is acceptable except to shape foot feather, or to remove feather between the pads or between the hock and the feet." This is an important point as the Sussex Spaniel is a natural breed and should not be overglamorized for the show ring.

Health Concerns

This breed has changed very little. Despite the small gene pool, there is a good record of producing sound, healthy dogs with few breed-specific problems. Be aware of the following:

- **Hip dysplasia:** The Sussex Spaniel is listed 8th in terms of breed incidence of the condition. From the dogs assessed, 41.9 percent were diagnosed with hip dysplasia (see page 22).
- **Entropion:** The construction of the eye, which allows some (but not excessive) haw, has led to an increased risk of this condition (see page 23).
- **Congenital cardiac conditions:** There is some incidence of heart murmur and other heart disorders, so regular checkups are advisable.

NEW CHALLENGES

Training a Sussex Spaniel to perform beyond his natural working capabilities should be regarded as a challenge. However, if you build up a good relationship with your Sussex, there is no reason why you cannot have a go at the canine sports that are available.

Hunting

The Sussex is still highly prized as a working dog. His distinctive way of working is valued by the specialist, particularly when it suits the conditions.

This is a breed that comes into its own when working in the thickest cover. He uses his well-developed sense of smell to find game, and his tendency to give tongue as he is about to flush is regarded as an asset when the dog is completely obscured from sight.

The Sussex tends to stick close to the guns and requires little in the way of formal training to work in the field. He is not a natural retriever, but with some work, he will become competent.

Obedience

This discipline does not really appeal to the Sussex, who is not one for slavish obedience. However, he can reach a perfectly acceptable level of training, such as is required in the good citizen tests (see page 10).

Agility

The Sussex is not built on athletic lines, and he does not move at a fast pace. However, he may enjoy the fun involved in agility training as long as it does not become too competitive.

Tracking

This is a discipline where the Sussex can excel. He loves to use his nose and has the determination and the stamina to keep going, even over difficult terrain.

Showing

The Sussex is not a natural show-off, although he can look eye-catching in the ring with his gleaming golden liver coat. Make sure your Sussex enjoys ring training, then he will be ready to cooperate when he comes before the judges.

Therapy Dogs

The scarcity of the breed means that there are few involved in this type of work. However, the Sussex has a cheerful and calm outlook on life, and with sensitive handling, he could prove to be an asset.

Karen Cottingham, of Primetime Sussex Spaniels in Maryland first took up obedience in the 1980s. Here she describes some of her experiences. . . .

"From the time I got my very first dog, I knew I wanted to do some kind of dog training. When I got my second dog, a Newfoundland, I knew I would need some very good training skills to control such a large dog, so I began attending obedience classes. I really enjoyed it, and within a couple of years, I was asked by my local kennel club to become one of the first people in my class to learn how to teach puppy kindergarten. There was a surge of interest among local dog owners in the area. Many people wanted 'professional' help to train their puppies rather than working purely from books or videos at home. It was the perfect moment for me to take my interest in obedience a step further.

"A few years after I'd begun teaching obedience, I got my first Sussex Spaniel. I loved Newfs because I have always admired breeds with 'substance' and bone. However, I wanted a slightly smaller breed with that substance, a breed that belonged to the Sporting Group. Sussex Spaniels fitted the profile in every respect.

"My first Sussex was Eadweard's Golden Bonanza, known affectionately as Anni. I mated her with a stunning dog called Snuffy (AKC Champion Sand Creek's Up to Snuff, Companion Dog, Senior Hunter, Best In Show winner, and Best in Specialty Show winner), and she gave me a litter of eight pups. Two of these, a bitch called Ch. Eclipse's Blossom and a dog called Ch. Eclipse's Snuffalupagus, became the foundation bitch and sire for my kennel—as you can probably guess, I was completely hooked on Sussex Spaniels by this time!

"In 1995, I mated Ch. Eclipse Snuffalupagus to an imported Sussex bitch from England, Oldholbans Lucy Lastic. The resulting litter included one of my star dogs, Miles (AKC Champion Primetime's FYI, Companion Dog, Senior Hunter). Miles is one of only four dogs to date to be awarded the Versatility Award from The Sussex Spaniel Club of America. Sussex Spaniels have a proud working heritage, but they are far less well known in the world of obedience. Miles has shown that it is possible to succeed at obedience as well as working skills and conformation.

Karen Cottingham with her obedience dogs. The Sussex is not a natural choice for obedience, but if a handler can tune into the Sussex mind, great results can be achieved.

"I really wanted to show that anyone can do obedience, no matter what breed of dog they owned, and Miles seemed to be the perfect choice to demonstrate that. Sussex Spaniels are not common in the obedience ring, but I knew he could do it if I was willing to work hard. Miles loves to 'play' to the crowd, and the moment when he achieved his Companion Dog Obedience title was one that will live in my memory for a long time. His title was proof that I was right, and it gave me encouragement to keep enjoying obedience with my dogs.

"Sussex Spaniels are just plain funny to watch in obedience, because they usually don't take it too seriously. However, they certainly enjoy the special attention, especially when they're applauded and cheered—they know it's all for them.

"I now have over a dozen conformation, obedience, and working titles bestowed on our Sussex Spaniels, which is proof enough that this highly versatile breed can adapt to almost anything. Sussex Spaniels make ideal pets because they are fun, low-maintenance, very affectionate, and adaptable.

"I'd recommend some level of obedience training to all dog owners. It increases the bond between dog and owner and results in a well-behaved, adaptable dog. It's all about starting off correctly. Ideally, you will own a puppy that shows interest in eye contact and attention, and you should start working on attention training and 'waiting' from an early age. However, never forget that each dog is an individual. If the dog does not seem to be enjoying himself, don't push it. It's not worth ruining your relationship with him by forcing him to do something he

Breeding dogs of sound temperament and socializing them is vital for both competition dogs and pet dogs.

does not enjoy. Just concentrate on getting the basics right by attending puppy kindergarten and the canine good citizen scheme.

"People often overestimate the difficulty involved in obedience training. It does require effort, but it is a lot of fun, and much training can be incorporated into everyday life at home. Positive reinforcement is the key—rewarding your dog for performing well encourages him to focus his attention on you and to respond to your commands willingly. By making training fun, you will not find yourself getting easily frustrated, you and your dog will enjoy yourselves, you will have a beautifully behaved companion, and you will have developed a strong bond."

CHAPTER ELEVEN

THE WELSH SPRINGER SPANIEL

Active, hardworking, and totally devoted, the Welsh Springer Spaniel, with his distinctive rich red and white coat, is not one of the most popular of the Spaniel breeds, but he has an enthusiastic following, particularly in his native home.

Bred to flush and retrieve game, the Welsh Springer was developed on similar lines to the English Springer Spaniel, but there are now significant differences between the two breeds in both temperament and appearance. The Welsh Springer is a most lovable breed but is more demanding than the English Springer. The Welshie is kind and affectionate, and he absolutely adores his family. He has a real need to be with his people at all times and will be unhappy, or even destructive, if he has to spend periods on his own. A lively, energetic dog, the Welsh Springer is slow to mature and will be playful and puppylike for a number of years.

In terms of appearance, the Welsh Springer is smaller and lighter than the English Springer. He is compact and symmetrical in build, and he is made for endurance. This is a dog who will never give up, even after spending a long day in the field, working in harsh conditions. His muzzle is not as full and deep as the English, and his ears are much smaller and vine leaf shaped, lying close to the cheeks. The glorious rich red color is a feature of the breed, and the silky coat lies close to the body. The Welsh has less feathering than the English, and so he tends to be easier to care for.

A merry, fun-loving dog, the Welsh Springer is still valued for his sporting abilities, but he has found his true niche as a loyal and loving companion who believes that the best treat in the world is simply to be with his family.

BREED HISTORY

The Welsh are tremendously proud of their native breed, which has an ancient history. It is thought that ancestors of the Welsh Springer may have arrived in Wales with the Gauls in pre-Roman times. There is certainly a marked similarity between the Brittany, who was

In Wales, the Welsh Springers are still known as "starters."

developed in France, and the Welsh Springer. By 250 B.C. there is evidence that Spaniels were being used as hunting dogs in Roman-occupied Britain. There is reference to the dogs' "springing" action, and Oppian, a Roman poet, gives a detailed description of a Spaniel-like dog.

In the Renaissance period, red and white Spaniels were used for retrieving—working with the falcon and with nets. There are a number of tapestries that show dogs with Welsh Springer coloring bearing a resemblance to the breed. These dogs were valued in the field, and although small in numbers, they were very much a part of the sporting scene until the 1800s. It was at this time that the liver and white and the black-and-white Spaniel found favor. These dogs, who later became known as English Springers, became far more numerous. It was only in a small area in Wales—in the Neath Valley—that the Welsh Springer was preserved. These Springers were often referred to as "starters" because of their ability to start or

spring game, and in Wales the breed is still known by this name today.

Separate Identity

With the advent of dog shows in the mid-19th century, people began to take more interest in different types of dog, and breeders were anxious to establish breeds in their own right. In the early days, the English Springer and Welsh Springer were shown in the same class as the only difference between them was color. Breed enthusiasts were keen to perfect the spectacular red coloring of the Welsh Springer, and this led to the two varieties becoming more distinctive.

One of the most influential early dogs was Corrin, born in 1883, and owned by Mr. A. T. Willams of the Gerwn Kennel. Corrin's parents were both red and white, and he was registered as a Welsh Cocker. When he bred to Mena of Gerwn, he produced Rover of Gerwn, who was an outstanding Welsh Springer and went on to become the breed's first champion. In 1902, Mr. Williams and other breeders gave evidence to the Kennel Club in England, and this led to the formal recognition of the Welsh Springer Spaniel as a breed in its own right.

Spaniels were imported to the United States in the late 1800s, and there were a number of red and white dogs among them. The American Kennel Club recognized the Welsh Springer in 1906. The first dog to be registered was Faircroft Bob in 1914, and five other dogs were registered in the same year. The breed looked set to become established in America, but it disappeared almost immediately. This was due in part to the two world wars, although the English Springer remained strong in numbers.

For whatever reason, there were no registrations of Welsh Springers between 1916 and 1948. It was thought that after the end of the Second World War, there were no Welsh Springers left in the U.S.

This situation was rectified when 11 Welsh Springers were imported in 1949. In 1952, Miss D. Ellis brought a team of five Welsh Springers to the U.S., and she showed them extensively. These dogs became the foundation stock for the breed in the U.S. With the help of a number of judicious imports, the breed became established on entirely British bloodlines.

THE WELSH SPRINGER SPANIEL TODAY

The Welsh Springer Spaniel has retained a stronghold in Wales and has a small following elsewhere in Britain. The breed is currently ranked 77th by the Kennel Club, with annual registrations of 362. In the U.S., the Welsh Springer has never caught on like the English Springer, ranking 113th in American Kennel Club listings with 291 registrations a year.

A small but select fan club has probably been of benefit to the Welsh Springer, which remains a breed without exaggeration and is very true to the original type developed by the earliest pioneers. The British Kennel Club and the American Kennel Club have drawn up their own breed standards, but in essence, they are very similar in their description of what the ideal Welsh Springer Spaniel should look like.

General Appearance

A compact, symmetrical dog—not leggy—who is built for hard work and endurance, he has

The breed's stunning coloring has attracted many fans.

substance without coarseness and is a quick and active mover.

Breed Characteristics

A breed that is ancient and pure in origin, the Welsh Springer is strong, active, and merry.

Temperament

A kindly, loyal, and affectionate disposition, the Welsh Springer may be reserved with strangers but he is never shy or unfriendly. He is a devoted member of the family.

Head

The head should be in balance with the body—not so broad as to appear coarse nor so narrow as to be racy. The skull is slightly domed with a well-defined stop. The cheeks are well chiseled, and the muzzle is of medium length and is fairly square. The nostrils are well developed and flesh colored to dark. The American breed standard emphasizes that the Welsh Springer's head is unique and should not approximate that of the other Spaniel breeds.

The Welsh Springer is strong and symmetrical in build—he should not appear leggy.

Eyes
Medium size, oval in shape, the eyes should not be sunken or prominent. The typical expression is soft. The color should be hazel or dark. Yellow or mean-looking eyes are highly undesirable.

Ears
Set at eye level, the ears hang close to the head. They are comparatively small, narrowing toward the tip like a vine leaf. They are lightly feathered.

Mouth
Strong jaws with a perfect scissor bite (upper teeth closely overlapping the lower teeth) that are set square to the jaws.

Neck
Long and muscular, clean in throat, and set into sloping shoulders.

Forequarters
The shoulder blade and upper arm are approximately equal in length. The upper arm is set well back, joining the shoulder blade with sufficient angulation to place the elbow beneath the highest point of the shoulder blade when the dog is standing. The forelegs are of medium length, straight, and well boned. The elbows are close to the body, and the pasterns are short and slightly sloping.

Body
The body is strong and muscular, with a deep brisket and well-sprung ribs. The length of body should be proportionate to the length of leg. The loin is slightly arched and muscular. He is well coupled.

Hindquarters
Strong, muscular, and well boned. When viewed in profile, the thighs should be wide and the second thighs well developed. The bend of the stifle is moderate, and the hocks are well let down.

Feet
Round, firm, and catlike with thick pads.

Tail
Well set on and never carried above the level of the back (although the American standard states that it can be slightly elevated if the dog is excited). A lively action.

Movement
Smooth, powerful, and ground covering, driving from the rear. When viewed from the front, the forelegs should move forward in an effortless manner.

Coat

Straight or flat, it is silky in texture and dense enough to be waterproof, thornproof, and weatherproof. It should not be wiry or wavy, and the British standard states that a curly coat is highly undesirable. The forelegs, hind legs above the hocks, and the underside are moderately feathered, and the ears and the tail are lightly feathered.

Color

Rich red and white only. Any pattern is acceptable, and any white area may be flecked with red ticking.

Size

British (approximate height): Males 19 inches (48 cm) at the withers, females 18 inches (46 cm). American (ideal height): Males 18–19 inches (46–48 cm), females 17–18 inches (43–46 cm).

LIVING WITH A WELSH SPRINGER SPANIEL

In many ways, it is surprising that the Welsh Springer is not more popular as he has a most engaging personality and is one of the easier of the Spaniel breeds to care for.

Family Situation

If you have to be out for long periods in the day, do not get a Welsh Springer! All Spaniels enjoy human companionship, but the Welshie cannot do without it. He is utterly loyal and wants nothing more than to be with his family at all possible times. Some owners find this behavior quite demanding, but most see it as part of the essential charm of the Welsh Springer Spaniel. He gets on extremely well with children, although it is important to ensure that games do not get out of hand, particularly when the Welsh Springer is young.

This is a friendly, outgoing breed who takes life as it comes and will adapt to city or country life as long as he is given sufficient exercise. A Welsh Springer will be perfectly happy to share his home with other dogs, and his response to meeting other dogs when he is out on walks is playful and uncomplicated. Aggressive behavior is completely alien to the breed. The Welsh Springer is also tolerant of small animals—once he is over his curiosity.

An alert watchdog, the Welshie is probably more reserved with strangers than the other Spaniel breeds. In most cases, this is a dog who acts before he thinks, but when the Welsh Springer is meeting strangers, he is surprisingly cautious. He tends to hang back and is wary

The Welshie insists on being included in all family activities.

Keep your puppy focused on training by using treats—this is a certain way to his heart!

rather than shy. Once he sees the strangers accepted in the family circle, he is more than ready to make their acquaintance and enjoys getting extra attention.

Trainability

Quick-witted, eager to work, and with limitless energy, the Welsh Springer really does need to have his mind occupied. Youngsters in particular have boundless enthusiasm for life, and this needs to be channeled constructively.

It is important to start training at an early age and to make it as much fun as possible in order to keep your dog focused and motivated. Remember, this is a breed that is slow to mature, and you will find that your dog's attention wanders if exercises are boring or repetitive. Break up training sessions with lots of play, which will help to use up some surplus

energy as well as encouraging the dog to interact with you. You will also need to work hard at socialization, especially in relation to meeting strangers, so that your dog's natural caution is not expressed by barking unduly.

Although your Welsh Springer will want to be with you all the time, make sure you teach him to spend short periods on his own so that he does not develop separation anxiety. This is a condition where the dog cannot cope when he is left alone and may bark continuously or become destructive. In severe cases, a dog may bite and lick his paws until they become red and sore. The Welshie needs to have confidence that you will come back so he will settle quietly on his own.

Beware of the Welsh Springer's Houdini-like qualities—he is remarkably agile and inventive when it comes to escaping. Climbing ladders, opening doors, and leaping over fences are all part of his repertoire.

Living with a Welsh Springer Spaniel is never dull—you can be certain that your dog will provide you with nonstop entertainment and the very special devotion that is unique to the breed.

Exercise

The Welsh Springer is a handy size, which means that he can live in a small house or an apartment, but his exercise needs must never be neglected.

The Welshie was built for endurance—and he really does keep on going. He loves to use his nose, and he spends every second of his walks following scents, quartering the ground, and then disappearing into the undergrowth. He will adapt to two or three regular walks a day rather

Agile and energetic, the Welsh Springer Spaniel thrives on mental stimulation combined with exercise. If a dog is not being used for work, you will need to provide an extensive program of varied outings. If you have access to a safe stretch of water, the Welshie will play retrieve all day.

than a long day in the field (which would be his natural preference), but the outings must be varied and stimulating.

The Welsh Springer is a natural retriever, and you can use up his energy by playing retrieve games. He is also an excellent swimmer, and if you have access to a safe stretch of water, he will enjoy retrieving from it. One thing you can be certain of, you will tire long before your Welsh Springer does!

Grooming

The correct Welsh Springer coat is flat and silky, with moderate feathering on the legs and body and light feathering on the ears and tail. The coat is dense. Compared with the other Spaniel breeds, it is relatively easy to care for, and two grooming sessions a week should be sufficient to keep the coat in good order.

Pet Dogs

• Use a bristle brush to groom the short body hair. You need to work through all the coat, but take care not to scratch the skin.

• A pin brush or a slicker brush can be used on the feathering.

• When you are confident that the feathering is free from mats and tangles, you can comb through it with a medium-toothed comb.

• If your dog is shedding, a hound glove is useful for getting rid of the dead hair.

• For pet dogs, trimming is restricted to the inside of the ears and the hair that grows between the pads. You may wish to make your Welsh Springer look a little smarter by trimming around his feet and tidying up the feathering on his ears and his tail.

Show Dogs

The American breed standard states that dogs should not have so much coat that it hinders their work as an active flushing Spaniel. In fact, this is rarely a problem with Welsh Springers, and show presentation is straightforward. It is important that the dog looks as natural as possible, and obvious barbering will be penalized in the show ring.

Feathering needs to be combed through to keep it free from mats and tangles.

- The finger and thumb method of stripping out hair is used on the top of the head and along the sides of the body.
- Surplus hair on the outside of the ears can be plucked out with finger and thumb, or you can use a trimming knife. Hair behind the ears and on the outer edge can be trimmed using thinning scissors.
- Thinning scissors are used to trim the hair on the throat, around the feet, and below the hocks. The tail can be tidied up, and if necessary, the hair on the underside can be neatened.

Health Concerns

The Welsh Springer Spaniel is generally hardy and healthy with few breed-specific problems. Check out the following:

- **Glaucoma:** This is not an uncommon condition in Welsh Springers, and all breeding stock should be eye tested (see page 23).
- **Cataracts:** This is of minor concern, but it is worth checking bloodlines (see page 23).
- **Hip dysplasia:** The Welsh Springer is ranked 63rd in the OFA's listing of incidence of the condition, with 13.9 percent of dogs tested diagnosed with the condition (see page 22).
- **Elbow dysplasia:** A ranking of 29th in the OFA's breed listing. Of the dogs evaluated, 5.3 percent were dysplastic—and all were Grade 1 (see page 22).
- **Thyroid conditions:** Research has shown that the Welsh Springer is ranked 10th for thyroid conditions. A study evaluating 66 dogs found that 81.8 percent were normal, 6.1 percent were suffering from autoimmune thyroiditis, and 3 percent were diagnosed with idiopathic hypothyroidism.

NEW CHALLENGES

Mental stimulation is a must for the Welsh Springer. He has proved successful in a number of disciplines.

Hunting

The Welsh Springer has a tremendous sense of smell, and he is tireless in the field, ready to work over all types of terrain. He has good bird sense, and his only fault is that he sometimes gets carried away with finding his quarry and forgets that he is working as a team. The Welsh Springer is not as fast as the English Springer, but he more than makes up for it with stamina. This is a breed where many dogs are still dual purpose, working as gundogs and also excelling in the show ring.

Obedience

This is certainly a challenge—not because the Welsh Springer lacks intelligence but because he is easily bored by repetition and will start to make up his own agenda. On the plus side, Welshies tune into their owners and like to please.

Agility

This sport suits the Welsh Springer's energetic and exuberant temperament. Handlers have to work at keeping the dog focused on the equipment and running a course, but many have achieved a fair degree of success.

Tracking

The Welsh Springer loves to use his nose. With motivational training, he will be ready to follow a trail, knowing his persistence will be rewarded.

Showing

Perhaps not the most fashionable of show dogs, the Welsh Springer still makes a striking picture with his spectacular red and white coat. Training should include lots of rewards so that the dog looks forward to going into the ring and shows himself off to full advantage.

Therapy Dogs

The Welsh Springer can be wary of strangers. With training so that the dog understands what is expected of him, he will make an excellent therapy dog. He is particularly good when working with children.

Welsh Springers are fast and quick to respond, which makes them first-class agility competitors. Make sure your Welsh Springer listens to you and watches out for your signals so you can steer him around the correct course.

Sally Abrahms, a writer from Massachusetts, spends her free time visiting a local nursing home with her Welsh Springer Spaniel, Isabella.

"I was introduced to therapy work when I was assigned an article on therapy dogs for the handicapped. Shortly after, I read about how they were being used to comfort traumatized families impacted by 9/11. I was intrigued and went on the Internet to learn more. Then I contacted Caring Canines, an organization in my area, to see if I could help.

"The group tested Isabella to determine if she had the right temperament for the job. She had to demonstrate that she could obey commands consistently, ride in an elevator, remain calm and steady even when bumped by wheelchairs and people, and was socialized enough to interact happily with other humans and dogs. No problem!

"Caring Canines send therapy dogs to a wide range of venues, including nursing homes, hospitals, schools, and shelters for victims of domestic violence. Isabella and I began our 'career' by visiting several nursing homes. One was a former monastery that cared for aged priests. At the time of our visit, it was near Thanksgiving and the room was decorated for the holidays, complete with a mammoth cardboard turkey. Isabella, ever the bird dog, was convinced the turkey was real and kept barking in a way that was out of character for this usually unruffled therapy dog! Had she taken the test in that room, she would have flunked! (We had to hide the big, fake bird.)

Sally and Isabella: The Welsh Springer is kind and gentle—and he loves people—so the breed is ideally suited to therapy work.

"After visiting a myriad of different nursing homes, I came to realize that I wanted more continuity. I wanted to go somewhere I could get to know the residents and staff and they could get to know us, so now I visit just one nursing home. Some of the residents have Alzheimer's and dementia, so Isabella and I always have to be reintroduced when we arrive and often several times during the short visit. They seem to visibly relax around Isabella. One woman talks about the two Schnauzers she used to own, and a man from Japan, who speaks no English and is quiet as a result, laughs and grins as he pets her. A woman, paralyzed in her left hand from a stroke, is absolutely thrilled when I place her hand on Isabella and she feels her soft ears.

"Some of the other residents are perfectly lucid and just need help to look after themselves. I think our visits offer the residents a break from their normal routine. It allows them to reminisce about the beloved pets they once had and to appreciate the unconditional love an animal provides. It is a nice break for the staff, too, and Isabella appears to love the attention. She also gets to do something out of the ordinary. Being a therapy dog teaches her patience and obedience—and the chance to perform her applause-proof rollover trick. I love the way she behaves when we make a visit, and I appreciate her all the more for it.

"Excuse the cliché, but therapy work is rewarding. It doesn't take much time on my part, about once a month for 30 minutes, and I know Isabella gives enormous pleasure to the residents. Even if I'm just deluding myself and what we do doesn't make that much difference in the long run, it still makes *me* feel good!"

The unconditional love offered by dogs lies at the heart of therapy work.

GLOSSARY OF TERMS

BRISKET: The forepart of the body below the chest, between the forelegs.

CHISELED: A clean-cut muzzle and foreface.

FLANK: The side of the body between the last rib and the hip.

FLEWS: Upper lips that are pendulous, especially at their inner corners.

HAW: Exposed third eyelid in the inside corner of the eye.

HOCK: The collection of bones of the hind leg that form the joint between the second thigh and the metatarsus.

HOCKS WELL LET DOWN: Hock joints close to the ground.

LEATHER: The flap of the ear.

LOIN: Region between the last ribs and the hindquarters.

OCCIPUT: Highest point at the back of the skull.

PARTI-COLOR: Variegated in patches of two colors.

PASTERN: The region of the foreleg between the carpus (or wrist) and the digits.

ROAN: A mixture of colored hairs alternating with white hairs, e.g., blue roan, lemon roan, orange roan, liver roan.

SADDLE: Dark patch over the back.

SLOPING SHOULDER: The shoulder blade set obliquely or "laid back."

STIFLE: The joint of the hind leg between the thigh and the second thigh (the dog's knee).

STOP: The step-up from muzzle to skull.

TICKED: Small areas of black, flecks, or colored hairs on a white background.

TOPLINE: Line formed by the withers, back, loin, and croup.

TUCK UP: The underline of the body curving upward from end of rib to waist.

UNDERCOAT: Dense, soft coat concealed by the topcoat.

WITHERS: The highest point of the body, immediately behind the neck.